A Companion
to Shakespeare

The Non-Shakespearean
Elizabethan Drama:
An Introduction

Robert P. Adams

University Press
of America™

Copyright © 1978 by

University Press of America, Inc.™

4710 Auth Place, S.E., Washington, D.C. 20023

ISBN: 0-8191-0540-6

Library of Congress Catalog Card Number: 78-58821

To

Marjorie

CONTENTS

Preface

The aim of this essay is to increase the reader's enjoyment and understanding of literature and life, in the English Renaissance and hopefully today, through bringing him into intimate contact with the vigorous, many-sided dramas written by Shakespeare's brilliant contemporaries. No widely-held assumption about the non-Shakespearean drama is wider of the truth than is the notion that, from Kyd and Marlowe to Jonson, Webster, and Ford, all the playwrights are intelligently to be read as pale imitations of Shakespeare. Rather they strike off in many directions, into often piercing inquiries into human nature, expressed in resourceful plays of varied but often high poetic quality. While the enormous and obviously deserved reputation of Shakespeare grows, his contemporaries--now that the sentimental excesses and inhibitions of 19th and early 20th-century romanticism are fast waning--are coming more and more back into their own. In England, in American university theatres, in drama festivals in the parks of major cities, from New York City to Ashland, Oregon, and occasionally on television, one has an opportunity to enjoy staging of some of these non-Shakespearean plays from time to time. And the intelligent reader can always enjoy staging them for himself in the imagined theatre of his own mind. Moreover Shakespeare himself can be the better enjoyed for knowing his competition.

A reader will want good texts of the non-Shakespearean plays, and these are readily available in several paperbacks. I recommend *Elizabethan and Jacobean Comedy: An Anthology,* and *Elizabethan and Jacobean Tragedy: An Anthology,* both edited by Robert Ornstein and Hazelton Spencer (both paperbacks; D. C.

Heath, 1964). In addition, because the text in the
Tragedy is inferior, one separate play is strongly
suggested: George Chapman's original *Bussy D'Ambois,*
ed. Maurice Evans ("A New Mermaid"; Hill & Wang,
1966). For convenience I shall refer to the *Comedy*
and *Tragedy* anthologies by the short titles, or as
O-S.

With this guide and these three paperbacks, the
reader may look for some richly varied and challeng-
ing entertainment.

Foreword

On Elizabethan Drama Exclusive of Shakespeare

Many readers and play-goers who enjoy English
Renaissance drama only through their acquaintance
with Shakespeare tend to assume that his genius was
representative of his great age in the drama. A
parallel assumption is that all the other playwrights of about 1585-1630 really sought to do what
Shakespeare did, only, not being Shakespeare, they
fell short of his accomplishments. If all these assumptions were true, there would be little lost in
simply concentrating wholly on Shakespeare and virtually ignoring his extremely diverse colleagues and
competitors.

The plain fact is, however, that virtually none
of the other playwrights--those who are the focus of
this guide--had any demonstrable intention to imitate
Shakespeare. (There is perhaps one exception--The
Thomas Heywood who wrote the touching un-heroic
domestic tragedy, *A Woman Killed with Kindness* in
1603, about when Shakespeare was writing his romantic
and very heroic tragedy concerned with marital in-
fidelity, *Othello*.) Of course many of the dramatists
living in Elizabethan-Jacobean London were aware of
each other's work, and doubtless they often learned
something from it. But the beginning of a greatly-
expanded pleasure to be drawn from the rich drama of
Elizabethan England is to free one's mind, as far as
possible, from preconceptions or assumptions strictly
relevant to Shakespeare. Hence, as far as possible,
the approach taken here will be to view each play and

its writer on his own terms. Comparisons and contrasts to Shakespeare will not wholly be excluded,
of course, but the contrasts are far more apt to be
enlightening. Thus with Dekker's *Shoemakers'
Holiday* (1599), Jonson's two racy London comedies,
Every Man in His Humor (1598) and *The Alchemist*
(1610), Beaumont's gaily farcical *Knight of the
Burning Pestle* (1607)--in all these we may explore
ranges of the comic spirit which are set down in
finely individualized styles.

In the broad realm of tragedy, the non-Shakespearean writers are even more strikingly seen to be
(as the current phrase goes) "doing their own thing."
Thomas Kyd's *Spanish Tragedy* (*ca*. 1585) is not only
a driving play of passion and ill-fated ambitions
but the rugged father of a whole host of so-called
revenge plays, even including *Hamlet*. More deeply
studied, it is a drama of man's endless search for
justice on earth. With Christopher Marlowe's *Doctor
Faustus* (*ca*. 1590-1591) we encounter one of the few
great innovators in modern tragedy. Some acute
historians (e.g., Preserved Smith, *History of Modern
Culture*, Vol. I) see the Renaissance as most distinctive for its explorations of the brave new world of
the sciences. And Marlowe's intensely forward-looking
imagination concentrates on the central figure of a
supreme scientist who envisions limitless power to be
achieved through radical forms of knowledge which
many conservative Elizabethans regarded as black and
devilish arts. Both of these powerful tragedies of
course antedate Shakespeare entirely. With George
Chapman's original version of *Bussy D'Ambois* (written
1600-1604), we encounter the pioneer in the modern
tragedy of passion versus reason. Indeed some aspects of the play (for instance, the 5th act torture
of the heroine by her self-righteous husband) con-
spicuously foreshadow the mid-20th century's so-
called 'theatre of cruelty,' more rightly perhaps
described as the theatre which dramatizes man's persistent inhumanity to man. After Chapman, we shall

come to John Webster's lurid tragic vision in *The White Devil* (1611-1612), written about when Shakespeare had left active theatre-work. Drawing on quite recent actual Italian history, Webster shows us a drama of mingled horror and beauty which seems to suggest that the old once-heroic devil-figures had become superfluous and that God was at a far remove from human affairs; for he shows how modern man is triumphantly able to create his own hells on earth. With Middleton & Rowley's *The Changeling* (*ca.* 1622) and John Ford's *The Broken Heart* (*ca.* 1632), we shall reach the end of our present journey through many different worlds of the comic and the tragic. Some squeamish critics have long cried 'decadent' at these three last plays. I rather see them as deep and often strongly moving inquiries into the nature of modern men and women, so often ruled more by their fundamental emotions than by so-called 'reason.'

Along this line of dramatic study, moreover, the reader who delights in rich and rare language will have a fine opportunity to enjoy a wide variety of individualized styles. If in the end he returns to Shakespeare, I suggest that even that extraordinary writer will be more complexly and rightly enjoyable than he is when isolated from the mainstreams of creative energy and imagination which make the entire Renaissance drama in English one of the most memorable happenings in all modern literature.

I *An Induction to English Renaissance Comedy*

Persistent Aspects of the English Comic Spirit

Generally in this approach to the spectrum of
drama which excludes Shakespeare as far as is feasible, I suggest that the happiest way toward enjoyment and sound understanding of comedy is to try to
divest one's mind of assumptions and preconceptions
derived from Shakespeare's plays. Or, when it is
most useful, to approach non-Shakespearean comedy,
as well as tragedy, as though Shakespeare never wrote
for the theatre. Artificial as this method is, it
may prove to have solid merit. For one thing, it may
free a student of laughter, or of the view of the
human race as a comic spectacle, as *comédie humaine*,
from unconscious enslavement to the notion that
Renaissance comedy can wisely be seen as the result
of an orderly sort of evolution, supposedly duly reflected in surviving literature. This curious notion
of evolution, reflected in many histories of the
drama, frequently seems to operate on the implicit
belief that the natural climax and almost the aim of
this assumed process, in comedy, was Shakespeare's
romantic shows done in the 1590's, leading up to such
brilliant creations as *Twelfth Night* or *As You Like
It.*

I rather suggest that you take a broad view of
the English comic spirit over the two centuries
before the great Elizabethans came on the scene--a
broad view that considers all material for humor and
comedy, regardless of the *literary form* in which it
may have appeared.

1

Such a brief sketch, hardly a survey, does suggest that the major tendency of English comic writers is more often toward some kind of salty, satiric, down-to-earth form of realism than it is toward escapes from reality into imagined worlds of more or less pure romance.

One may well begin with Chaucer's grand *comédie humaine*, for the *Canterbury Tales* is the first masterpiece in the language to deserve such a subtitle. Not that Chaucer was averse to romance. When he chose, he could do it beautifully and do it straight (e.g., the Knight's Tale, or the Wife of Bath's story of what women desire most, or the lovely Prioress' delicately handled tale of the boy-martyr, Hugh of Lincoln). Chaucer's humor can be polite, but it can also be very rough and, at times, even brutally satiric (as in the ending of the Pardoner's tale, when that finely self-portrayed crook tries to 'con' the pilgrims, only to be smashingly put down by the usually genial Host, Harry Bailey).

Yet what most readers remember with the greatest pleasure, I suggest, is the richly flavored gallery of highly credible men and women of his age. Saints are few, sinners plentiful. Clever rascals abound, then as now trying to live by their wits with as little honest work as possible. The Miller is fairly a brute, and Chaucer sets him down candidly. The Wife of Bath, that past mistress of the "old dance" of amour, is splendidly brought to life, in all her honest vulgarity and intense vitality.

On balance, moreover, Chaucer is content to tell the truth about human nature as he saw it. And although he is obviously aware that social corruption was in plentiful supply between about 1385 and 1400, he is really no would-be social reformer. Rather he energizes one's sense of the joy of life. Over his whole show there plays a lively sense of comic irony, which

usually derives from a shrewd perception--a kind of
'double vision'--that what men and women pretend to
be is often comically different from what they are
beneath the social masks they wear. (As we all are
guilty of this double standard, the comic awareness
is borne in on the reader of Chaucer.) Some of his
best characterizations--this is very English in its
humor--are indeed of expert rogues; and while neither
Chaucer nor his reader need be duped, both may enjoy
seeing the expertise of rascality as part of the
comedie humaine.

     Oddly enough, part of the late-medieval comic
scene appears in a contemporary of Chaucer's who *is*
very much the would-be social reformer. For it begins
to seem that English humorists dare to be somewhat optimistic about the potential capacity of men and women
to survive their own follies. Satiric laughter may
help toward self-cure? *Piers Plowman's* author is
still in doubt, but his poem gains some of its hard
strength through its rugged and popular satiric humor.
Phonies and crooks, particularly in the church, are a
favorite target (as they were of Martin Luther a little
over a century later). The literary *form* of *Piers
Plowman* is, ironically, a dream-vision. But the flavor
and content are anything but dreamily escapist. The
comic and satiric effect is often powerfully down to
earth.

     Even high romance, in Chaucer's England at least,
had begun to show comical aspects. We still do not
know the exact identity of the brilliant contemporary
of Chaucer's who wrote *Gawain and the Green Knight*
(about 1385). But there is no doubt that he had a
splendid sense of satiric humor and even, in some of
the romance's most dramatic scenes, of sexy comedy.
To many, the rambling tales of King Arthur and his
more-or-less noble knights of the legendary Round Table
were of durably high-epic seriousness. (Even the almost humorless John Milton at one time considered doing

3

an epic on the Arthurian material, before he fixed on
what became *Paradise Lost*.) Poor Sir Gawain! He
comes before us, early on, as virtually the ideal
knight. Alas! as the story of his varied adventures
unfolds, he well earns his laughable comeuppance.
When tempted by the first notable comic *femme fatale*
in our literature, he proves only too fallible--proves
indeed to have a winningly human desire to stay alive.

The laugh is on him in the end, and when he is
honest enough to tell the assembled Knights and Ladies
of the Round Table how he made an unheroic fool of himself, the hall roars with genial laughter. But the
humorous effect shows Gawain descending from the
heights of fantastic would-be perfection. He rejoins
the human race, and we can laugh heartily as we wish
him well. For in his shoes, would we have done any
better, if as well? Matter of romance has been blended with a salty kind of realistic observation of men
and women as they are. It appears that the developing
English comic spirit tends to fuse a measure of idealism with a large share of something like a form of
realism. Another way of looking at it suggests that,
very early, Englishmen began to see that in this life
the tragic and the humorous must coexist and do so
vigorously, in a healthy literature.

Those somewhat acquainted with classical drama
criticism, more or less derived from Aristotle, know
that the Greeks thought of comedy and tragedy as completely unconnected entities: comedy can have no right
place in tragedy, and vice-versa. Our sketch of the
English comic spirit, however, already shows that many
very English writers, as their work makes evident,
thought this artificial separation unnecessary if not
false to their observations of human nature. With
sturdy honesty, they tend--very refreshingly, too--to
"tell it like it was." Neo-classically educated men,
like Sir Philip Sidney about 1583, of course mightily
deplored what to them was a gross defect, the English
persistence in mingling tragic concerns with jigs and
hornpipes. So much the worse for such over-intellec-

tualism, and so much the better for both English
comedy and tragedy of the high Renaissance.

So far, we have glanced at the comic spirit as
it chanced to find expression in non-dramatic literary
form. But by the last part of the 14th century--say
1385-1400, the 'age' of Chaucer--or early in the 15th
century, some vigorous staged drama already thrived in
England. I mention two famous examples, in both of
which matter for laughter is fused with pious and
tragic themes. Now best-known of all "morality plays"
is *Everyman* (*ca*. 1485; see *Tragedy*, pp. 252-264). Occasionally staged by college actors to this day,
Everyman is at times ironic, at other times poignant,
but always it focuses on lasting qualities of mankind.

The central character, Everyman himself, has some
affinities with Arthur Miller's Willy Loman in *Death
of a Salesman*, which is a kind of morality play for
our own time. Everyman, like Willy, has ridden a wave
of seeming prosperity, a glad-hander surrounded by
fair-weather friends. Then, to Everyman's comic in-
credulity and real dismay, the boom is lowered. Death,
a character not to be tricked, makes it clear to Everyman that his time has come, his own death is really
imminent, and he must make the dread last journey
alone--unless he can get some old buddy to go with him.
Everyman asks his good-time-Charlie friends to go to
death with him.

Hastily, they all desert, much to his silly surprise. The character of Good Deeds *is* willing, but,
ironically, is too starved to walk (in other words, as
the parable goes, Everyman has, before this crisis,
conveniently forgotten to do any Good Deeds to speak
of). The comic spectacle is that of a worldly-wise
man whose supposed wisdom is really his major folly in
disguise, so that he ends up falling on his face in
the net of lies, deceptions, and fraud that he has unwittingly made for himself. But Everyman does in the
very end (like Willy Loman) regain a measure of human
dignity and even a flawed self-respect when he know-

ingly undertakes the inevitable, to meet his death as best he may.

We have taken this much time to discuss this ruggedly built little late-medieval morality play, because in one form or another it has reappeared throughout the later history of English and American drama. Underlying it is the persistent idea of the world as a battleground between forces of right and of wrong. This idea may be too simple, but it still has enormous popular appeal. For instance, what major American politician fails to try to present to the voters the image of the battler for right (his party) *versus* wrong (the other parties)?

Surely we must notice the curious and touching idea of comedy embodied in the late-medieval "Second Shepherd's Play," in which rough low farcical humor is skilfully blended with serious piety. The low comedy lets us see, realistically, very believable English shepherds as they detect a wily sheep-stealer Mak, and his guileful wife, Gill. When the outraged shepherds, seeking a stolen lamb, arrive at Mak's hovel, Mak tries to 'con' them all with the idea that his groaning wife has just delivered a baby. But the 'baby's' too-black nose protrudes from Gill's grimy bed-clothes, and a summary search reveals that she has 'delivered' a stolen lamb. Farcical uproars! Whereupon news arrives of the Christ-child's birth, and they all troop off in good humor to pay Him their pious homage and present their humble gifts. All being penniless literally, they give a cluster of cherries, a live bird, and Daw charmingly offers a tennis ball for "thy hand small." Mary thanks them all graciously, and they exit singing.

The "Second Shepherd's Play" is memorable on several counts where the English comic spirit is concerned. First is its adroit mixture of poetic styles: the poet skilfully makes use of rough country talk for the shepherds and the sheep-stealing farce, then suavely moves to a tone of tender lyricism for Mary. In the second place, this little play was originally part of the great cycle-dramas staged at the Corpus Christi festivals in many medieval English towns. Magnificent in their broad conception, these cycle-plays staged the entire drama of mankind as set down in the Bible. Divided into stageable episodes, the action began with Creation and ended, perhaps several days of play-watching later, with the Judgment Day.

To the English medieval mind, this whole affair was a special kind of comedy. For, after all sorts of vicissitudes, "fallen" man in the grand windup has a *happy ending* (at least happy for the saved, if not for the sinners). For medieval Englishmen thought a 'comedy' told a story which began badly but ended happily. Such an idea of comedy may seem strange to us, but it made major sense to them. Hence a Dante could title his great narrative poem--not at all a stage play--"The Comedy," and others soon made it "The Divine Comedy," for it began in Hell and ended in Paradise. No one could imagine a worse start or a finer ending!

One other brief remark about the cycle-plays, of which "The Second Shepherds' Play" was originally a part. In the epic drama from Creation to Judgment Day, the whole imagined universe was seen as a battleground in which forces of evil (embodied in Satan, the supreme Devil that American Puritans labeled 'Old Nick') fought it out with God and his angels. The prize was the soul of mankind. But of course, according to the Biblical account, God was bound to win in the end. And obviously Satan was equally bound to *lose*. The logical result was that in the medieval cycle-plays, Satan became a kind of mighty but *comic* figure. Vastly cunning, he could be depended on to think up ever new tricks and devices to entrap mankind. But the faithfully Catholic medieval audience was sure Satan could not win. Hence they could and did laugh hugely at him. Later on, in Renaissance tragedy (and even some comedies), queerly gay devilish villains appear. (Shakespeare's figures of Richard III or of Iago are such villains.) And some critics think, perhaps rightly, that these medieval

7

comic backgrounds help in part to account for such
light-hearted rogues. As for the medieval Corpus
Christi cycle-plays, they actually lasted well into
the 16th century. Indeed they were only dying out in
provincial towns when Shakespeare (b.1564) was a boy.

The coming of the Renaissance in England (*ca.*
1475+) very markedly enlarges the spectrum covered by
the English comic spirit. Old forms of humor persist.
And notable new forms appear, destined to change English comic views of life for centuries, perhaps until
our own late-20th century time of transition. Briefly
we may identify the most probing of these new early-
16th-century views of humor as Tudor New-Humanist.
And we closely associate them historically with the
names of Sir Thomas More (of *Utopia* fame) and with
England's greatest scholarly and witty guest (of *ca.*
1500-1517), Erasmus. These New-Humanist varieties of
humor and satire are so rich that we can here do little more than try to epitomize them. Basically, they
create by historically and culturally reaching far
back in time and literature, to contrast what man has
made of life on earth with what he could make of it--
particularly when the potentialities of developing
science are taken into account. The implied question
is simultaneously comic and tragic: if western European mankind at least has the knowledge and abilities
required to live a 'good life' on earth, here and now,
why are we currently in such a mess?

The comic spirit seems to flourish when varying
ideas of a 'good life' are put forward but seem to be
in conflict. The resulting differences of opinion
tend to create lively views of the possibilities--the
perhaps happy beginnings if not endings--that may
await mankind, given the requisite degrees of social,
economic, and political organization. The wide range
of such human potentialities is variously explored in
such works as Erasmus' *Praise of Folly* (written in
England, 1509; published 1511); in More's *Utopia*

8

(1517), with both its destructive and constructive
satire; in More's *Epigrams* (see *The Latin Epigrams,*
tr. Bradner & Lynch, Chicago, 1953); in many of
Erasmus' *Colloquies*, including the anti-war *Charon,*
which were read and translated well into the 18th
century; and in many lesser writings.

A tremendous contribution to modern ideas of
comedy was made when More and Erasmus reintroduced a
major sense of irony into man's views of the potentialities of life. To oversimplify a contrast, such
medieval men and women as are characterized in Chaucer's pilgrims making their slow horsy way to Canterbury, had before them no alternative to the world-
wide Catholic view of the human condition. That is,
this life is necessarily miserable for most men; and
their only hope for the better lies in an after-life.
But with the Renaissance, here symbolized by More's
Utopia for England, there was advanced the radical
(and comic) idea that men can, if they use their wits,
create a good life here and now, during their own
lifetimes and those of their children.

This whole New Humanist search for a good life--
as seen broadly in the work of More and Erasmus--rad-
ically altered the perspectives for both comedy and
tragedy. Comedy tended thereafter to become a search
or struggle for happiness--a pursuit, as Thomas Jef-
ferson put it. Comedy might henceforth reach a
'happy ending' when the drama demonstrated to the
audience an idea of realistically achievable happiness. Inversely, tragedy tended--after these New Hu-
manists--to become a tragedy of human *waste.*

But in all this brief sketch of the English comic spirit, as it appears in some of the literature of
two centuries before the flowering of the drama in
Renaissance England, there is no steady straight-line
development, no really clear pattern of what deserves
to be called an evolution. Sir John Skelton was a
contemporary of Erasmus and Sir Thomas More. But
Skeltonic humor, while an authentic part of the total

9

pre-Elizabethan comic brew, is almost traditionally low-comic. Yet Skelton was in his own way also a renaissance humanist! The Chaucer of the rowdy Miller's Tale would have delighted in Skelton's tavern humor, seen in "The Tunning of Eleanor Running." The Eleanor in question keeps a drinking-place for poor people and makes her own beer out of highly unsavory ingredients. No matter: the poor people flock in, and accordingly Skelton gives us a vividly realistic panoramic view of the lot. It would appear that the English comic spirit still remained heartily hospitable to low life and its manners, or lack of them. All remain part of the *comedie humaine*.

The mix of elements tending to express the English comic spirit grew, in a very irregular, bouncy sort of way, as the Renaissance of the 16th century developed. Of course in England, to which the Renaissance came so late, it is strange to see the Reformation at work at the same time. Medieval students enjoyed arguments, so once we had a versified debate between Body and Soul. Some Tudor humanists, including John Rastell and John Heywood, both related to Sir Thomas More, experimented with "Interludes" for private staging; and these sought to entertain not so much through highly emotional scenes or flowery description as through lively action and witty dialogue. The characters are only two or three; Heywood's methods sometimes show traces of old French farce; these early writers have not yet mastered the art of setting a complex action on stage. "Character" in these interludes tends to the familiar social types: husband, wife, priest; the wise man and the fool. But, as T. Brooke notes, Heywood achieved "naturalness in entrances, exits, and stage business beyond anything previously seen in English theatre."

By about the first years of Queen Elizabeth's long reign (1557-1603), the comic spirit in England had attracted considerably sophisticated talent. The durable English delight in rough-and-tumble humor shows up in the often amusing and ingeniously written,

10

as well as quite stageable, farces: Nicholas Udall's
[*Ralph*] *Roister Doister* (*ca.* 1553) and Mr. S's *Grammer Gurton's Needle* (*ca.* 1562). Humanistic school-
masters turned out these shows. They had read their
Plautus cheerfully (as Shakespeare did before he stole
the ideas for his early *Comedy of Errors*), and they
would have enjoyed, as Broadway audiences did in the
1960's, the Plautine mishmash billed as *A Funny Thing
Happened on the Way to the Forum*. My point is that
even these early Elizabethans read their minor Roman
classics (Plautus), but then used their dramatic and
comic wit to set on stage laughable and unromantic
visions of down-to-earth *English* life. They were not
trying to find romantic *escapes* from reality but rather to master dramatic ways of *transmitting* some parts
of everyday reality, via their comic vision.

What is more, Elizabethan humorists, before the
great age of the drama (1585+), show ranging interest
and skill in setting before the reader, before the potential playgoer, credible contemporary speech and
manners, or behavior. By 1575 that man of many talents, George Gascoigne, had entertained and even partly scandalized some courtiers with his witty narrative,
'realistic' in its broad effect, which first was printed in 1573 as "The Adventures of Master F.I." In this
piece, told through letters, verses, and interspersed
ironic commentary by an onlooker-type, we watch a long
Elizabethan country-house party pass before our eyes.
The comic hero, F. I., fancies himself to be irresistible to the sophisticated Lady Elinor, but in the end
she makes a fool of him. Only he is the last to
realize as much, although almost everyone else in the
story, as well as Gascoigne's readers, could see the
amusing debacle coming all along.

Gascoigne, tremendously versatile in literary experiment, also adapted late Roman comedy (which tends
to broadly farcical and rowdy low humor) in his witty
and dramatically well-structured *Supposes*,* the first

*See *Supposes* in *Comedy*, ed. Ornstein-Spencer,
pp. 287-315.

prose comedy proper in English, based on the indispensable, shrewd observer of elemental human nature, the merry Roman Plautus. Gascoigne's comedic work is one literary jump away from the young Shakespeare's first go at rowdy, 'realistic' farce, seen in *Comedy of Errors* and *Taming of the Shrew* by the early 1590's.

Indeed, a major tendency of the whole Renaissance in England shows in a bent toward acute and often unromantic observations of men and women as they are. By the 1510's, Brant's version of the *Ship of Fools* was delighting Englishmen: in this we imagine a great ship traversing England and laugh at the huge variety of human folly as the fools rush aboard. (Such a travel-framework story permits showing the reader a wide panorama of human nature. By the 18th century when the novel develops strongly, it takes on durable and deserved popularity, recognizable in Fielding's often uproariously comic *Tom Jones*. Again, in the 1960's, it appears in Katherine Porter's wryly hard-bitten and ironic *Ship of Fools*.) To the Elizabethans, the realistic humor of low life was part of the broad comic scene, as appears often in A. Judges' collection, *The Elizabethan Underworld* (1930), in Robert Greene's pretended exposes of petty criminals in London (the 'cony-catching' pamphlets—a 'cony' is a "sucker" in our slang), and in Thomas Dekker's droll *Gull's Hornbook*.

But this sketch of the workings of the English comic spirit has reached, with such names as Robert Greene and Thomas Dekker, men who actually wrote with great skill for the popular Elizabethan theater of the 1590's. By then the inventive talents of Englishmen had conceived and built working public theatres where sophisticatedly-written dramas could actually be produced.

Our sketch is almost ended. But we must observe the comic sides of two great writers not usually considered for their humor: Thomas Kyd of *The Spanish Tragedy* (*ca*. 1585); and Christopher Marlowe himself,

12

as in parts of *Tamburlaine*, or *The Jew of Malta*, or
Doctor Faustus. These are pre-Shakespearean plays.
With these dramatists, of course, we have reached the
great age of the Elizabethan drama proper. And it is
remarkable to see the range and power of the humor
(sometimes light, sometimes mock-epic, mock-heroic,
macabre, or ferocious) which they present as an authentic part of their insights into human nature. In
The Spanish Tragedy, for instance, the professional
murderer Pedringano, who has been condemned and stands
on the gallows, fancies himself safe and jests gaily
because he thinks his political protector has secured
a last-minute pardon which is in a box waved before
him by a smiling boy. But we know, as the boy does,
that the box is empty! The highly influential and intellectual critic, T. S. Eliot, could see and enjoy
what he exactly epitomized as Marlowe's "farce of the
savage old English humor" in Marlowe's *Faustus* (*Selected Essays* 1950 ed., pp. 104-105).

In all fairness, however, this view of the English comic spirit reflected in literature of two centuries before the heyday of the high Elizabethan drama
must pay some respects to the persistence of what may
be termed "romanticisms." For in the 1580's, at the
court of Queen Elizabeth (a very special kind of non-
public audience indeed), the exquisitely nonrealistic
little plays by John Lyly were all the rage. You have
a fair example in *Endymion*, in *Comedy*. Characteristically, Lyly invented never-never lands, apt to be
imaginative projections of ancient myths or fairy
tales, peopled by thin figures, hardly "characters,"
who speak an often-fantastically stylized, if playful
and moralized, language. A minor court-politician as
well as playwright, Lyly was careful to see that the
comedies were liberally sprinkled with recognizable
compliments to Queen Elizabeth and her favorites.
These small-scale plays of Lyly's were a special taste
then, and they certainly are so now, to put it mildly.
Hazelton Spencer's comment seems fair:

Nothing could be more sharply in contrast
with the robust drama of [Kyd and] Marlowe
than this bloodless and overliterary play
[*Endymion*]. Had the Jacobean masters followed the lead of [Lyly] instead of culti-
vating the coarser but livelier entertain-
ments of the popular theatres, the greatest
triumphs of the greatest age of English Drama
would never have been achieved. Nonetheless,
Lyly exercised a salutary and civilizing influence on Shakespeare and his colleagues.
It was not instruction in the human heart
they needed so much as the example of a considered style. The drama of passion might
be powerful, but it was too often crude and
flamboyant. If Lyly's writing is precious
in its euphuism and anaemic in its avoidance
of strong emotion, it is a virtuoso prose,
and the delicacy of its flavor is not without
a certain charm. Prattled by little boys
[the actors] it was probably more amusing to
a fastidious audience, unused to grace in the
theatre, than it seems to us, who expect it.
(*Comedy*, p. 2)

Learning his playwright's trade, the young Shakespeare,
at least, mastered Lyly's kind of thing along with many
other styles, while he was searching for his own voice.
(See the word-games played in his *Love's Labor's Lost*,
for example.) And *Midsummer Night's Dream* owes some of
its exquisite atmosphere to Lyly's art.

Shakespeare himself speedily enough left somnolent
Stratford to make fame and fortune where they could
best be made, at the power-center of London--and England's dramatic and literary center as well. But,
ironically, Shakespeare's special form of romantic
comedy, perfected in the 1590's, never throws any light
on the London which he must have known intimately. His
peculiar great talent seeks to make the exotic and far-

distant seem, for the play's duration, entertainingly credible. The action is typically supposed to be in Padua or nearby (*Shrew*), or in a somewhat fanciful and quite 'literary' Italy (*Merchant of Venice*), or in a fantastical let's-pretend English countryside (*Midsummer Night's Dream, As You Like It*), or in a quite off-the-map Illyria (*Twelfth Night*), and so on. In short, all these belong to his particular world of the 'romantic.' Even when, as in the grimly funny *Measure for Measure* (1603), probably by then influenced by Ben Jonson's salty London realism, he looks at the seamy side of city life, it is not his London but an imagined Vienna that we are led through. Master finally of his kind of comic world, one of generally "sweet" and "romantic" concerns, by the end of the 1590's he had virtually completed, as Muriel Bradbrook noted, his contribution to a "stable form of Elizabethan comedy" (*Growth and Structure of Elizabethan Comedy*, p. 5). Yet in the nature of this remarkable creation, it had few successful later growths, and even Shakespeare himself found it imperative to make radical changes after about 1600. That is, after Ben Jonson had already carved out bold realistic pathways to London comedy by his 1598 success with *Every Man in His Humor*.

*   *   *

I have tried to suggest a broad view of the English comic spirit as it appears in a wide variety of surviving literature, from the time of Chaucer to the beginning of the great Elizabethan drama with Kyd and Marlowe, just before Shakespeare appeared on the London theatrical scene. A study of these works reveals little evidence of any clear evolutionary pattern whose resulting end product would necessarily be the kind of stage 'romantic comedy' familiar to us in Shakespeare's plays such as *Midsummer Night's Dream, Merchant of Venice*, or *Twelfth Night*. The broad tendency is rather toward a kind of mixed realism, occasionally colored by romantic elements. Increasing-

15

ly, the writers are concerned to exhibit men and women
as they saw they were, and as alert audiences themselves could verify by their own experience that they
were. The broad movement, in short, is toward a kind
of comedy centered on London life--"London comedy"--
in which, as Ben Jonson defined it in the Prologue
to his 1598 show (in which Shakespeare acted a part),
the aim is to represent imaginatively:

> . . . deeds and language such as men do use,
> And persons such as comedy would choose
> When she would show an image of the times,
> And sport with human follies, not with crimes. . . .
> (Comedy, p. 103)

Romance and Reality of Everyday London Life
Thomas Dekker's *The Shoemakers' Holiday* (1599)

Tom Dekker, in his masterpiece *The Shoemakers'
Holiday* (produced in 1599) and Francis Beaumont in his
ingenious mock-heroic and burlesque *Knight of the
Burning Pestle* (probably 1607) belong firmly to the
richly varied, imaginative world that is London comedy.

"Sir," said Dr. Johnson to his crony Boswell, as
they stood happily in the center of the 18th-century
London swarm, "when a man has tired of London, he has
tired of life." And, "Sir, within five miles of where
we now stand, there is everything that makes life
worthwhile." To such true lovers of cities in their
endless social variety, the country is a bore. "Sir,
when you have seen one blade of grass, you have seen
them all."

Making cunning use of 'romantic' materials, both
these comedies are memorable for the vividness of
their realism, and for what may fairly be called their
Dickensian humor. Both make good use of at least
double-level plots, by which two or more stories are
told on stage in an intertwined progression. Both
good-humoredly celebrate London middle-class business
success stories. The real hero of Dekker's comedy is
not any one of the traditionally great aristocrats
(King Henry V or the crusty Sir Hugh Lacy, Earl of
Lincoln). The finest dramatic inventiveness is rather
shown in his figure of the irrepressibly middle-class
(or downright working-class) Simon Eyre, a master
shoemaker who gets rich speedily and winds up as a
fun-spirited Lord Mayor of London. With him come vividly on stage his vain, fat wife, Margery, and a whole
breezy crew of down-to-earth London trade-union men,
the shoemakers Roger, Firk & Co., who are cheerfully

joined by the head-over-heels-in-love draft dodger, Rowland Lacy (who plays AWOL to stay near his beloved Rose, in or near London; pretends to be the Dutchman Hans, and who luckily gives Simon Eyre the hot business tip that leads to his sensational business success and eventually to the Lord Mayorship).

Early on, we meet young Rowland Lacy, who is supposed to take his troops to France for patriotic glory. (These same French wars of King Henry V had, in 1599, but recently been celebrated by Shakespeare.) But the alleged glories of foreign invasion are of no special interest to Dekker. Instead, war's realities are illustrated by the fate of poor Ralph, a journeyman shoemaker who is drafted, marched away lugubriously, and returns later on, a permanent cripple. (However, the 'romantic' plot-twists, finally, if with tongue-in-cheek improbability, reunite him at the church, with his ever-loving Jane, just as she was about to give up all hope and marry another man, the quite decent Mr. Hammon.) Hazelton Spencer rightly observed that "This is a play of romantic plot curiously allied with realistic manners, the first so charming and the second depicted with a gusto so nearly Chaucerian that the combination is irresistible. Simon Eyre [who stoutly intervenes on the side of honest young love] wins every reader's heart as easily as he wins the King's." For this comedy-King Henry V is himself so moved by the winsomeness of honest young love that he pardons the AWOL and strictly-speaking traitorous Rowland Lacy, placates the old curmudgeons (the Earl of Lincoln and Sir Roger Oateley, former Lord Mayor of London), and puts his overwhelming blessing on the play's happy ending.

Dekker's *Shoemakers' Holiday* (1599)

When and where, if it is not purely a myth, did the fabled "merry England" exist? Some would say, in literature; it is the stuff of Shakespeare's romantic comedies of the 1590's, and with these they might include the comic underplot in the *I-II Henry IV* plays. But we have observed that Shakespeare never centers his actions on Elizabethan London; he never writes "London comedy." Of course fat Sir John Falstaff, Prince Hal & Co., in the epically-scaled *Henry IV* pieces, frolic at the Boar's Head Tavern in London's Eastcheap slum. But these splendidly-drawn figures are all wrapped up in an heroic play about right kingship, rebellion, high politics, and the already (by the 1590's) almost played-out world of medieval chivalry and its martial honor. This was already old-fashioned stuff, and only Shakespeare's genius could give it a brief spate of renewed life. In Dekker's *Shoemakers' Holiday* we also hear of the Boar's Head Tavern (p. 76; III.i.85-100), but no longer do romantic madcap princes while the time away there. Simon Eyre, himself of almost Falstaffian comic proportions, met his wife Margery when she was a tripe-seller in Eastcheap (hardly a romantic occupation), and Eyre sends his boy to the Boar's Head for beer to pacify his workmen during one of their periodic threats to quit en masse when fat Margery's nagging gets them down.

I suggest that Tom Dekker, far better than Shakespeare apparently cared to do, brings to dramatic life the spirit of "Merrie England." In *Shoemakers' Holiday* we may enjoy both the humor and the pathos of a fascinating London that may once have existed before the Puritans (like the dour Malvolio of Shakespeare's *Twelfth Night*) and their kill-joy philosophy took most of us over!

Who is so hard-hearted as to deny that the trials and tribulations of young lovers are always, in every age, meat for comedy? But are they the *only* such meat? Are all possible comedies really only variations on the theme which is lightly tossed to the audience early in *Midsummer Night's Dream*: "The course of true love never did run smooth"? In Shakespeare, we might think so. Not in those masters of the London scene: Dekker, Beaumont, and above all, Ben Jonson.

In *Shoemakers' Holiday* the world of comedy broadens out to include a whole steamy, sweaty, mostly unheroic sweep of everyday London life. Sophisticated lords and ladies now have relatively minor parts. Dekker weaves his plot to celebrate the humor and even the workaday romance of trade union life, and--in the career of Simon Eyre--the fun of achieving worldly success without losing one's *joie de vivre*. Not just love, but love and money make this world go round.

Dekker's plot, with masterful ease and seeming naturalness, spreads its exposition lightly over the first two acts. By their end, themes of humor and of grief are in motion on the stage. Two contrasted pairs of lovers are engaged in the energetic pursuit of happiness, against some longish odds (Rowland Lacy and Rose; the humble shoemaker Ralph and his plain Jane). But of equal if not greater interest is the fun with which Simon Eyre pursues business success: he loves his workmen as sons and esteems shoemaking the finest of trades; he puts down his fat shrew of a wife, Margery; and he is quick to sense a rare chance for quick wealth. One might argue that Simon Eyre, the master shoemaker who comes on so strongly, larger and gayer than life, is himself a key figure in a new and more modern kind of 'romance.'

The two sets of lovers have their individualized joys and woes. The young hero of the comedy is a dashing prodigal, Rowland Lacy, who has recently lived it up grandly during a travel year financed by his toughly kind uncle, the Earl of Lincoln. Returned, cheerfully broke, to London, Lacy, with a keen and democratic eye, has become so enamored of the Lord Mayor's (Sir Roger Oateley's) charming daughter Rose, that he dares to desert his command to the French wars in order to hide in London to court her. It is worth noting that when Lacy ran out of money abroad, he turned his wits to work by learning the shoemaker's trade in Germany. Here is a hero who does not scorn honest manual labor (in contrast to the 'romantic' Bassanio of *Merchant of Venice* who, having spent his inheritance, borrows from the generous Antonio in order to finance a hunt for a rich heiress).

For Dekker, the Lacy-Rose love affair brings on stage two fine minor comic characters, the vividly Elizabethan father, shrewd middle-class Sir Roger Oateley, who pits his wits against the equally sharp Earl of Lincoln, Lacy's uncle-as-substitute-father. The Oateley-Lincoln side of the plot shows us a very Elizabethan contest of matchmaking, which is also only too clearly one of money-making. (Dekker is nothing if not true to life here, for in common Elizabethan practice, when autocratic fathers ruled the roost, true love tended to come in a poor last as a motive for marriages.)

Counterbalancing the more refined lovers is the working-class pair, Ralph and Jane. Newly-wed and honestly but simply in love when we meet them, they are grievously separated when Ralph is taken as a draftee for the French wars (supposedly in the London company in which Rowland Lacy is to have a command). Loyally, Simon Eyre, a good protector of his shoemakers, tries to get Ralph a deferment. When he fails (page 69), all the shoemakers give Ralph a grand sendoff, while poor Jane weeps. The dramatic lot of this humble but very believable pair of lovers gives the play some of its realistic pathos and tenderness.

But where are the villains? So far, in Dekker's plot, none has appeared. I suggest that none ever does appear. (This is in sharp contrast to Shakespeare's usual comedic reliance on some concentrated embodiment of evil, some "villain"--like the improbable Shylock in *Merchant of Venice*--to create the obstacles which must be overcome if a happy ending is to be achieved.) Does Dekker's comic world of *Shoemakers' Holiday*, like the

21

world of today's modern society, dispense with the
stage villain as one more hackneyed relic of an un-
realistic notion of life, derived partly from fading
"romances"?

The point may be clarified by the contrast between the Sir John Falstaff of Shakespeare's *Henry IV*
plays and the superb Dekkerian comic invention that is
Simon Eyre, master shoemaker and finally Lord Mayor of
London. Each is splendidly fat. Each can be exuber-
antly gay. Each has a style of wit and humor distinctively his own, so that their speech can be confused
with that of no one else in their plays. Each is
ambitious to shine in the world. Neither suffers fools
gladly.

But Falstaff, who in some ways is the villain, the
would-be seducer of the Prince, belongs to a peculiar
form of the Shakespearean-imagined universe of men, one
linked more closely with the medieval past than with
the modern present (1600+). Falstaff is at least a
double man--one foot in the low-comic underworld of
Eastcheap, one foot more precariously in the great and
heroic world of kingly power politics. As long as he
is shown on stage in the company of Prince Hal, Falstaff
shines with incomparable humor. Take away the Prince
from Falstaff (as much of *II Henry IV* does) and the
general consensus is that he is by no means such fun.
Falstaff and women? There are the somewhat greasily
comic scenes in which he makes fools of Mistress
Quickly and his favorite whore, Doll Tearsheet. Falstaff and men other than Prince Hal? There is relatively minor fun to be found in his dealings with the
generally weak-witted characters whom he gulls for
lack of better. We suggest that Falstaff as much as
his beloved Prince Hal belongs to a special kind of
Shakespearean romantic and heroic universe of men.

We would not push too far the contrast between
Falstaff and Dekker's characterization of Simon Eyre

in *Shoemakers' Holiday*. But we think a fine piece of humanity is imaginatively set before us in II.iii (*Comedies*, pp. 72-75) and in III.i (pp. 76-78). Simon Eyre and his wife, fat Margery, are a better comedy pair than Falstaff and Mistress Quickly. The ancient marital war-between-the-sexes has rarely been staged more drolly than in the running combat between the working class hero, Simon Eyre, and his fat, foolish, nagging shrew of a wife. In III.i (pp. 76-78) a terrible comic crisis threatens, for Dame Margery has nagged the journeymen shoemakers intolerably and they all threaten to quit in disgust. (In the Elizabethan style, they live where they work.) Challenged, Simon Eyre comic-heroically shows what it is to be master in one's own house and workshop. He "loves his work-men as his life"--fat Margery blubbers as she is put down--Eyre denounces her silliness--and the crisis is nicely resolved as Eyre placates his men also by send-ing out to the Boar's Head for some beer at his expense. So all is cheery again--and done in vivid Elizabethan everyday speech which makes ours of the late-20th century seem pallid by comparison.

Dekker's comic vision indeed suggests that the rising, business-like, and traditionally unromantic working-class and middle-class folk of England are sometimes delightful in their own right. Yet Simon Eyre is only a master shoemaker, and his little open-fronted workplace and home on Tower Street is a million comedy miles from the heroics and high power-politics dramatized in Shakespeare's *Henry IV* or *Henry V* plays, or in the curious Tower prison chamber scene in which the deposed King Richard II broods in a political vac-uum on how to compare his prison with the great world outside.

Moreover, Dekker's comic vision is projected in a variety of poetic styles quite his own. Critics like to call him "Dickensian," but he beats Dickens by three centuries. He avoids the high and sometimes toplofty or heavily heroic style (e.g., as seen in Shakespeare's

23

King Henry IV's rebuke to Prince Hal, or in Hotspur's wild essays on honor: "pluck bright honor from the pale-faced moon"). Rather Dekker expertly matches his style to his men, to men of his London. Thus the horny-handed shoemakers are Cockneys all, given to the vivid, rough, slangy language of the London shops and streets. Often this speech is bawdy, as the shoemaker Firk so often is. These Cockneys are shrewd, canny, given to practical jokes, delighting in playing witty deadpan games at the expense of the pompous would-be 'great' men of the world. Patriotic enough as Englishmen, the shoemakers rise above mere nationalism in devotion to their "gentle craft."

Firk is the most precisely-drawn of the workmen; for Dekker's comic mode in representing him, see especially IV.v.53-to end of scene; pp. 90-91. Late in the action, Sir Roger Oateley, formerly Lord Mayor (before that, a rich grocer), is disgusted that his daughter Rose has run away with "a foul drunken lubber, swill-belly, / A shoemaker"! Unluckily for him, he says this in Firk's presence. That honest shoemaker fires up to make a cunning defence of his craft and to lay a comic trap into which the pompous Sir Roger and the Earl of Lincoln promptly fall. (Each, for different reasons, wishes to balk the runaway marriage of Rose with Hans/ Lacy.) The Cockney Firk, whose like may readily be found on London's streets today, pretends to be stupid and transparent. "God's nails," he says to them blandly, "do you think I am so base to gull you?" (IV.v.131).

He first sends them hot-footing it to St. Faith's Church to break up the Rose-Lacy elopement. Then, with us, he chortles (p. 91) to think of the fine comic foul-up that is sure to result. For while his shoemaker-buddy Hans (Lacy in disguise) and Rose "chop up the matter at the Savoy" (get a quickie marriage), the wealthy gentry will be over at St. Faith's. There, we know, Ralph's wife Jane (who believes Ralph killed in the French wars) is about to marry another gentle-

24

man (the eccentric Mr. Hammon). So Firk cheerfully anticipates that Sir Roger will try to break up *that* would-be marriage instead of his daughter Rose's. "Oh brave! there will be fine tickling sport."

Dekker's women have a lively and psychologically-authentic part in his comic panorama in *Shoemakers' Holiday*. Rose is the more genteel of the two young heroines, the more ladylike and well-bred. When we first meet her she is already in love with the handsome young spendthrift officer, Rowland Lacy, and the reader might forgivably take her for a pallid romantic figure such as the docile Hero of *Much Ado About Nothing* (1598-1599), or the naive, polite Juliet as she appears to us before she falls with deep seriousness into her luckless love for Romeo. But this Rose is a vigorously lifelike young woman of London, courageous and spunky. She puts up a clever fight for the man she has her heart set on, and in the end she nicely outwits her well-meaning, domineering businessman-father, who thinks arranging a marriage is no more complicated than any other business deal.

When we first meet Rose (II.i; p. 71 in *Comedy*) she is imprisoned at her father's Old Ford place, brooding on her beloved Lacy, and weaving a flower-garland. Her Cockney maid, Sybil, who saw young Lacy marching off to the French wars, has toughly practical advice for her mistress: Forget him! "Let him go snick up [go hang]" (p. 72, 1.61). Not our Rose. Made of sterner stuff, she rather bribes Sybil to find out for sure whether Lacy actually has left for France. Will Sybil do this spywork for Rose's "purple stockings"? Will she! "By my troth, yes . . . I'll sweat in purple, Mistress, for you. . . . Oh, rich! a cambric apron! Faith, then have at 'up tails all!'"

Rose further shows her charm and good worldly sense in the skillful way with which she fends off the decent but above all wealthy businessman, Hammon. His wooing of her is honest, but she gets rid of him with both

courtesy and spirit (III.iii, p. 79). Indeed she is
more than a match both for Mr. Hammon and for her
blundering father, Sir Roger Oateley. Incidentally,
note the fine comic touch in Sir Roger's quick emotions when Mr. Hammon quits the game of wooing. On
the one hand, as a businessman himself, Sir Roger is
disgusted that his daughter seems to have such poor
financial judgment! But he is equally disgusted with
himself at his own failure:

> Fore God, I would have sworn the puling girl
> Would willingly accepted Hammon's love;
> But banish him, my thoughts!

And with comic speed he turns his attention to the
next order of the London day's business, the rare
quick-profit deal he has worked out with Simon Eyre
over a 'hot' shipload of highly saleable merchandise.
And he will sweeten this deal and make further profit
by making Eyre Sheriff. This is no heavy father of
romance, no elegant aristocrat with his head full of
whimsies. Rather Sir Roger is a London man of his
time who is brought deftly to life before us through
Dekker's comic art.

Rose is indeed no aristocrat or Platonic-romantic
heroine at all but, as her father calls her, a "fine
cockney" (p. 84, 1.56)--a true London lass. The irresistible Simon Eyre gives her splendid advice on choos-
ing a man (p. 84, 11. 59+): ignore "courtiers"--
rubbish, no men at all! Since you're ripe for a man,
rather "marry me with a gentleman grocer, like . . .
your father; a grocer is a sweet trade--plums, plums."
Of course if Eyre himself had a daughter, he would bid
her "pack" if she married any but an honest shoemaker,
like himself! "What, the gentle trade is a living for
a man throughout Europe, through the world."

Among Dekker's women, fat Margery Eyre, formerly
a Cheapside tripe-seller, now Eyre's shrewish wife, is
a minor comic masterpiece of characterization in her

own right. She is a bundle of silliness. When she
nags Eyre's beloved workmen intolerably, Eyre denounces her in a fine brawl-scene and heaps praise on
his men, whom he treats as sons (III.i, pp. 76-77).
As Eyre gets rich and begins swiftly to rise in the
business world, turning his shop over to his men as
he becomes first Sheriff, then Mayor, then Lord Mayor,
what happens to fat Margery is comically a joy to be-
hold. Success ruins her fishwife charm. By gradual
degrees, she puts on false airs, as false as the
hideously gaudy and elaborate new clothes which she
thinks truly befitting to an important politician's
wife. Her 'bum' was huge to begin with, but since
vast bustles were in style, she must and will enlarge
it with one. She tries to drop her native coarse and
cockney vocabulary (by p. 81), and instead she begins
to mouth absurdly high-toned terms which she does not
really understand.

All this to the great, honest disgust of the
down-to-earth workmen, Hodge and Firk. But their
bluntly satiric mockery washes off fat Margery like
water off a duck. Speaking in a put-on "puling" voice,
she practices ghastly, mincing, supposed high-society
mannerisms of speech and action before us. Not content
with turning herself into a comic disaster, she feels
duty-bound to try to ruin Simon Eyre too! If they are
to be entertained by the Lord Mayor himself (high
society!), Eyre, she says stoutly and stupidly, must
"learn now to put on gravity" (III.v; p. 83). Will
success ruin Eyre? The momentary fine comic suspense
is dissipated in a roar of good humor, as Eyre scoffs
gloriously at his fool-wife. She can make herself
ridiculous if she likes, but he will go right on enjoying life in his own original ways.

A fine Dekkerian comic-pathetic insight into humanity, one involving fat Margery's rising vanity with
the fates of Jane and her Ralph, comes just before this
last episode. In III.iv (p. 81), Dekker, with acute
realism and candor, shows the unromantic truth of what
wars do to some men. For we see poor Ralph return

27

from France, crippled for life. Honest Hodge and
Firk, who have taken over the shoemakers' shop along
with Hans (or Rowland Lacy in disguise), greet the returned veteran with manly respect and sympathy, and
they offer him a job and their help. As for honest
Ralph, his whole desperate and heartbroken yearning
is to find, if she still lives, his "poor heart," his
lost bride Jane. During Ralph's colloquy with the
shoemakers, fat Margery has had her mind totally on
the fine new clothes she is going to wear now that
Eyre is Sheriff and they are rich. Page 82, lines
111+ are worth close reading. The honest workmen are
deeply sorry and embarrassed--they simply have no idea
what became of Jane. Then fat Margery speaks up--all
the while on stage perhaps looking in a hand-mirror,
patting herself, primping, imagining her new clothes,
bustle, French hood, the whole bit. Not even noticing
at first that Ralph has begun to cry from sheer heartbreak, Margery is completely indifferent, only absorbed
in her own selfish vanity. Offhand, she tosses out the
news that she simply disliked Jane and got rid of her.
Then, with amazing but true-to-life surprise she asks:
"But, Ralph, why dost thou weep?" Dekker's satire on
her is dead on target and managed with beautiful dramatic economy. Yet we can see that her thoughtlessly
cruel vanity is as authentic a part of humanity as is
Ralph's heartbreak and the pathos surrounding his whole
condition.

For Dekker's brilliant comic vision, seen in this
episode, sensitively presents true pathos without going
soft, or over-sentimental in the worst sense, or ex-
aggerating toward melodrama.

This power to present delicate relationships can
be grasped by seeing how Dekker puts before us, in one
exquisitely done little scene (IV.i entire; pp. 84-86)
the character and predicament of both Mr. Hammon and
of the comedy's lesser heroine, the Jane for whose loss
Ralph wept. IV.i shows us a Mr. Hammon who, already
rejected by Rose, seeks a wife for love, not wealth.

(This last, by the way, marks him as something of an eccentric in his age; he tells us he already *has* wealth enough.) The scene begins, dramatically, on a workaday London street where Jane has her poor little seamstress' open-front shop. Hammon, as his whole part in the play gradually reveals him, but without harsh satire, appears as one of life's losers when it comes to love. He himself sees the miserable irony of all this and shows it in the pensive soliloquy which opens the scene, when he tenderly watches Jane at work as she spreads out her little stock of handkerchiefs, bands, ruffs, etc., through whose sale she hopes to make a tiny decent living on her own:

> . . . I am infortunate:
> I still [=always] love one, yet nobody loves me.
> I muse in other men that women see
> That I so want!
> . . . such is love's lunacy. (IV.i.6-19)

He seems fated, as it were, to starve in the midst of plenty. And yet he is shown to be a decent, honorable man, almost entirely.

Follow this little comic scene of IV.i, taking in its implications. It could easily have been hoked up, made cheaply sexy or over-sentimental. But not in Dekker's comic vision! We the audience, by this point in the action (via III.iv), of course know that Jane's soldier-husband Ralph has returned, a cripple who seeks her everywhere in the maze of London. Jane only knows that Ralph seems to have vanished when with the English army in France: 'missing and presumed dead'? Moreover, Dekker implicitly requires that the audience bring its own common knowledge of humanity to this scene. That is, we know what the Janes of the world, then and now, know--what any sensible, still-young and pretty but very poor woman must know, namely that many wealthy men regard her femininity as a commodity, as much on sale as the ribbons Jane spreads on her sale-counter.

His soliloquy over, Mr. Hammon approaches. Jane
cries her wares, hoping for some sale. This comically-
clumsy but (as *we* know) honest wooer pretends interest
in a few things. Then he smiles with affectionate
tactlessness: "All cheap; how sell you then this
hand?" (i.e., herself). With grave, slightly sad dig-
nity--something it is not too easy for a poor girl,
alone, to hold on to--she quietly replies, "My hands
are not to be sold." Now of course this remark, with
her conversation to line 40, *could* seem a cheaply
flirtatious come-on. No fool, Hammon knows as much.
If she chooses to, Jane, no fool either, can clearly
understand all Hammon says as part of a game of would-
be sexual seduction on his part. Hammon moves to pro-
test that "I love you." (Does she shake her head--
'no,' 'I don't believe you'?) He says his feeling for
her is "true love"; why does she "hate" him? Keeping
grave courtesy (I think she *is* sorry for him), she
repeats: "What, are you better now? I love not you."
Hammon grows both more ardent and more despairing, as
he moves to a direct proposal: "I love you as a
husband loves a wife. . . ." Jane's reply (p. 85,
lines 58-66) beautifully sets before us a piece of the
hard truth of life as this poor, lonely woman sees it.
She regards him with kindly pity, not anger or contempt. She simply detests "witchcraft" (1.66), that
is the dirty little catch-me-if-you-can games that
many men and women do play against each other. With
touching plainness, she tells Mr. Hammon the whole
simple truth of her persisting loyalty to her lost
husband Ralph, who even now she dares to hope may be
alive.

Then comes a surprising psychological turn of
events, for with him Mr. Hammon has a printed list of
those killed in the French war, and Jane's husband's
name is there (11. 80-99)! Reading it, her heart
breaks, and she weeps heavily, hopelessly, in sheer
despair. And Hammon, moved by affection for her, is
moved to weep *with and for her* (11.92-125), as the

indicated action goes. Even as she rejects him and
wishes he would leave her alone in her grief, her deep
natural need for comfort moves her to respect his sympathy. I suggest that by about l. 95 he is weeping
too, and that soon she leans lightly against him,
hardly noticing his protective arm around her. Her
first wild outburst of grief works through to about
l. 99. Such grief is exhausting. Her sobbed requests,
that he leave her, grow weaker. Quietly clear, too, is
her real need for some man to love and protect her:

> Jane: 'Tis now no time for me to think on love.
> Hammon: [gentle firmness] 'Tis now best time for
>   you to think on love,
>   Because your love [Ralph] lives not.

Her successive 'nos' become weaker—less 'no,' more
'perhaps'? She suffers one last heavy stroke of grief
(ll. 113-122). Then emerges a discovery of curious new
half-truth: "If ever I wed man, it shall be you." Her
final line of mourning, "Death makes me poor," stands
in richly humane and ironic contrast to his hopeful,
"Thy breath hath made me rich."

    In all this finely-handled scene of IV.i in
Shoemakers' Holiday, there is nothing traditionally
romantic or heroic at all. These people are rather observed and set down with a candor and a psychological
truth that would not surprise us in a Chekhov three
centuries later. This kind of comic vision shows us a
realm of being with which Shakespeare is but rarely
concerned. The *Shoemakers' Holiday*, we suggest, is a
masterpiece of London comedy in its own right.

Recommended:

    Earlier comedies (in *Comedy*):

        John Lyly, *Endymion, The Man in the Moon (ca.
        1588)*, p. 1.

        Robert Greene, *Friar Bacon and Friar Bungay*
        (by 1592), p. 33.

31

George Gascoigne, *Supposes* (tr. 1566), p. 287.

Commentary:

Robert Ornstein, "General Introduction" to *Comedy* text.

Hazelton Spencer, "Introductory Note" to the *Shoemakers' Holiday (Comedy,* p. 66*)* and to *The Knight of the Burning Pestle* (p. 206).

Introductions in *The Dramatic Works of Thomas Dekker*, ed. F. Bowers (4 vols. Cambridge University Press, 1953-1961).

John Danby, *Poets on Fortune's Hill* (Faber and Faber, 1952)

Eugene Waith, *The Pattern of Tragicomedy in Beaumont and Fletcher* (Yale, 1932).

III   Unromantic Pleasures of London Life Today:

Ben Jonson's *Every Man in his Humor* (1598)

Jonson's Comic World and Vision

Not Shakespeare, but Ben Jonson, if any Renaissance writer deserves such credit, is the father of modern English comedy. But while both are greatly enjoyable, each man's comic vision is quite his own. They are by no means interchangeable. And the suppositions or preconceptions whose understanding aid enjoyment of Shakespeare simply do not fit or work for his friend and colleague in the London theater, any more than they do for such fine writers as Thomas Dekker of *The Shoemakers' Holiday* or Francis Beaumont of *The Knight of the Burning Pestle*.

We began this guide with a brief survey of the English comic spirit, seen in about two centuries of varied literature before the flowering of the drama after *ca.* 1585. The conclusion was that the major discernible tendency of English humor was toward a kind of lively mixed realism, at times colored by contrast with romantic elements. In short, toward vigorous shows based above all on London life, where the widest spectrum of humanity was after all to be observed and relished.

We re-emphasize these points because experience has shown us how readily readers and critics alike, often without noticing their own emotional and thought-processes, do indeed try to measure such splendid comedies as *Every Man in His Humor* or *The Alchemist* by what, for simplicity, we call 'the Shakespearean yard-

stick.' When we look in Jonson for the leading Shakespearean themes and attitudes, the plots, the char-
acterizations and the methods by which these are done,
for the uses of language ('style') whether in verse or
prose, and finally for Shakespeare's comic vision, we
do not find them. If instead we look at Jonson's art
on its own terms (the only fair way, after all), we
find Jonson a master comedist in his own right.

I can illustrate the elemental point--that Jonson
and Shakespeare, each a master in his own way, are radically unlike--and also show the kind of critical folly that all too commonly confuses the issues, by cit-
ing one major attempt to explain what is called the
evolution of *Elizabethan* comedy as rising out of a
conscious departure from the patterns common to such
late Roman comedy as that of Plautus, whom Shakespeare
doted on. Here, in tabular form, are the alleged differences:

ROMAN COMEDY	ELIZABETHAN COMEDY
Effect overall: Real-istic, sexy, satiric, earthy. The object is sex, not marriage (un-less men can be tricked into it).	*Effect overall:* All for love. The master-theme is some version of "The course of true-love never did run smooth." Lovers appear, struggling for happiness, with marriage their aim. Villains have the job of throwing obstacles in the lovers' way.
Plots: Are of cunning intrigue.	*Plots:* Tell of relatively simple stories of lovers and their wooings.
People:	*People:*

Many 'universal' social types, superficially un-
changed from age to age,appear and reappear. But there
are striking differences,and even the same old types,
in their updated forms,tend to assume altered qualities.

34

(1) The *old men* (*senex*) and their goatish folly. Very prominent. Satirized and gulled for "interests of gaiety."

(1) The *old men* "withdraw to the wings" of the theatre. If they remain, they are absurd but serious and are "gulled for gaiety."

(2) *Rascally men-servants:* Are prominent. They master-mind ingenious schemes.

(2) "Cunning servants survive mainly as native clowns." [The clown *was* an old tradition in England.] But the plots now deprive them of "opportunity for extensive scheming."

(3) *The heroes:* Are cynical young bloods "lusting for illicit liaisons" or "trafficking without delicacy for the possession of attractive concubines."

(3) *The heroes:* The 'romantic' hero who seeks the right wife, for love, becomes very prominent, as the young folks take the stage-center.

(4) *The girls:* Pursued by the heroes, they "flit across the scenes" as "mere accessories to the plot." They become our "personal acquaintances . . . only in direct proportion to their alleged impropriety."

(4) *The romantic heroine:* A rich stage-personality in her own right, she replaces the miscellaneous girls of late Roman comedy.

Theme of the play: It is sex, simple if not necessarily very pure.

Theme of the play: It is "love rather than sex." These lovers mean "honest matrimony." As compared with his sources, Shakespeare develops a "play of wooing," a love-game comedy.

35

All these contrasts are those of H. B. Charlton (*Shakespearean Comedy*, pp. 75-76 adapted). Not surprisingly, he finds the major clue to the development of what he calls Elizabethan comedy to be found in the 'new' hero and even more strikingly in the 'new' heroine. Now there is nothing especially wrong with Charlton's critique except one major thing. What he epitomizes is not rightly Elizabethan--much less Jacobean--comedy as a whole. Rather he describes that peculiar artistic invention which we know as Shakespeare's unique romantic comedy world (e.g., *Merchant of Venice, As You Like It, Twelfth Night*, etc.). And in *that* little universe, devised and ruled by his special comic vision, it is above all love that makes the world go round! Shakespeare's lavish art and above all his poetry is devoted to making this romantic universe seem believable and enjoyable, at least while we read or attend a well-acted production of his comedies. His art, however, often requires of the audience (as Coleridge acutely noted) much "willing suspension of disbelief."

In Ben Jonson's comedy London-life world of men, we may, however, speedily feel at home only provided we have some broad and reasonably sophisticated appreciation of modern city life as it often is. To quote a droll but shrewd advertisement for a leading U. S. stockbrokerage firm (Merrill, Lynch, etc.):

> At the risk of sounding cynical, we submit that it isn't love that makes the world go 'round. Being as romantic as the next brokerage house, we're reluctant to come right out and say what *does* make the world go 'round, but we feel we must. Actually, money does, though it's not usually considered good form to say so.

Rare Ben Jonson would have chuckled and agreed. Only he might have qualified the point by suggesting that money and *self-love* work beautifully together as master human motivations which power modern society.

To avoid confusion, let me suggest one definition of the society we call modern:

> By 'modern' is here meant the kind of
> society which is fairly cultivated, fairly
> comfortable, fairly complicated with
> classes not very sharply separated from
> each other, not dominated by any very high
> ideals, tolerably corrupt [note the 'toler-
> ably'; the intolerable may lead to tragic
> disaster], and sufficiently businesslike.
>
> (G. Saintsbury, *English Novel*
> [1919], p. 32)

Actually Saintsbury's view was first applied to 16th-century Italian society, which he found to have been then more modern than it had been until very recently. We suggest that, in a curious and very English, mud-dled way, the major aspects of such a modern society were appearing by around 1600 in London, the center of Jonsonian realistic comedy. And in the comic view of London life in *Every Man in His Humor* and in *The Al-chemist*, not so much love as money makes the world spin 'round most merrily.

Many of us should be able to find ourselves read-ily at home with Jonson's comic vision, for it comes close to paralleling the way a great many people really do view life, that is in terms of money, sex, or compe-titive rivalries. Or, in terms of a spirited search for Sustenance, Sex, Status, and Security. In short, between us and Shakespeare's 'romantic' comedy universe, there are bridges of special ideals which must be ima-ginatively crossed before we can enter and enjoy our-selves. But between us and Ben Jonson, there is no more a barrier of such ideals than there is between us and the world we find actually pretty much around us.

To this last generalization, however, I would make at least one qualification. For the toughly good-humored modern and realistic Jonsonian comic view of human nature does *not* fit the recurrent dark moods which have swept over Western society since World War I, moods in which some observers bitterly predict the imminent ruin of civilization itself by one man-made catastrophic means or another. Indeed at least one critic of old Ben Jonson's often hard-bitten and realistic comedy has asserted it to be, in broad effect, "so darkly deterministic that it precludes all possibility of [social] reform" (Harry Levin, in *Ben Jonson: Selected Works* [1939], p. 6).

Rather we hold to and suggest the idea that Jonsonian comedy humanistically and broadly celebrates human vitality and the sometimes unexpected power mankind develops to survive even its own follies. If society is to be or can be reformed, the methods are unlikely to be those of romantic escapism. T. S. Eliot wisely commented that:

> Of all the dramatists of his time Jonson is probably the one whom the present age would find most sympathetic. There is a brutality, a lack of sentiment, a polished surface, a handling of large bold designs in brilliant colours which ought to attract about three thousand people in London and elsewhere. At least, if we had a contemporary Shakespeare and a contemporary Jonson, it might be the Jonson who would arouse the enthusiasm of the intelligentsia. (*Selected Essays* [1950 ed.], pp. 138-139)

Jonsonian comedy does make strenuously cheerful demands on his audience (and of course even more on the reader, who must perforce try to imagine the play as it would appear before him were he in a theatre). But these demands in the main strongly resemble those which life-as-it-is also makes upon us when we try to understand and enjoy it intensely.

First of all he assumes his audience to be in its right mind and to be acquainted with--or at least interested in--the vivid passing show of civilized life

in a great metropolis. The people we meet in his
comedies are not exotics, though they may be eccentrics, a different matter. Neither are they larger-
than-life heroic. (Othello, for instance, is both
exotic and heroic, and so we must accept him to be.)
Counterparts of Jonson's characters are indeed generally fairly recognizable by anyone tolerably well
acquainted with life in a great city.

Further, Jonson assumes his audience to be fairly
familiar with the more usual patterns of social living
in modern society. We are supposed to know the *mores*,
to know the common forms of vice and folly which may
assume an endless variety of disguises or social masks.
We are presumed to know the main drives which spur men
and women on in their pursuit of happiness here and
now. More subtly, Jonson expects us to be aware of
the important role played by 'manners.' That is, by
the unwritten codes of behavior, the formal patterns
(even if outwardly informal, as so often now) which
sane men take for granted as the basis of civilized
society living under law. We may observe that, to
make comedy even possible, such a society observes a
tacit unwritten kind of social contract, according to
which, however violently we may come into conflict, we
agree not to murder each other.

Jonson's plots frequently appear to be extremely
ingenious, and they are. Yet what is most to be enjoyed is the masterly way in which he makes plot seem
to evolve directly from the dynamic interplay of character and situation. As life does, his plays move
from conflict to conflict. Rarely if ever do his characters, in their dramatic actions, violate what we can
recognize as normal probabilities in motivation or
psychology. (In contrast, Shakespeare adheres to the
idea of a play as a story told on the stage; whatever
basic improbabilities or unlifelike absurdities the
given story may contain, we are supposed to accept without quibbling; and his characters frequently do, in his

plots, not what we know they probably *would* do in life-as-we-know-it, but rather what the plot *requires* that they must do.)

With Jonson's comic vision, therefore, there is little or no call for the famous "willing suspension of disbelief" which the critic Coleridge found so indispensable for the enjoyment of Shakespeare. Jonson's aim is to make life-as-it-probably-is strongly manifest to our senses, especially to our senses of the humorous and the satiric. His comic vision rather *compels belief* in human nature, realistically observed and acutely set down.

Jonson's language--his 'styles'--beautifully supports this down-to-earth comic vision. It is only rarely lushly poetic, or literary, and only then because the plausibilities of the given situation and character rightly afford the opportunity. As, for instance, they do at the outset of Jonson's *Volpone*, when that lustful rich old fox gives, in beautifully-wrought verse, a word-picture of the glory and joy that vast wealth makes possible to a true expert in living, a magnificent connoisseur like himself.

Another grandly funny and lushly 'poetic' sequence of writing comes in *The Alchemist*, II.i-iii, a continuous sequence (*Comedy*, pp. 159-163), where the self-infatuated Sir Epicure Mammon (middle-aged, fat, greedy and foolish-wise) comes to the mock-scientific alchemist laboratory on the day when he really expects to receive the fabulous "philosopher's stone" which will enable him to turn any base metal into pure gold. To the skeptical Surly, who (rightly) suspects the seemingly pious alchemist, Subtle, to be an absolute cheat, Sir Epicure Mammon lets his sensual imagination run riot as he describes what he will do with all the wealth that is so soon to be at his command. What is notable about Ben Jonson's control of language here is that every word is exactly in character for the absurd Mammon.

Stylistically, in Jonson's best comedies, the text is, as it should be, inseparable from the tightly-woven web of motivation and action. All these are grasped and enjoyed together by the reader who has learned to relish Jonson on his own terms. There are no lengthy speeches which, however elegant or interesting for their own sake, are beside the relevant point of the immediate dramatic situation or character--something by no means uncommon in Shakespeare (several of Hamlet's soliloquies could serve as examples of such seeming irrelevancies). In Jonson, in page after page, as in the furious quarrel between some prize rogues, with which *The Alchemist* begins, the short lines of his realistic dialogue work to build the fabric of this robust and deeply English comedy. It is unusual for a single line to be wasted. First sketching in broad outlines, this comic master fills in the picture with rapid brush-strokes.

Jonson, as a broadly critical observer of modern man-in-society, is nearer than anyone else in English to Moliere. But he is less restricted in his scope. Jonson's focus is the rising middle-class, and he writes for them as one of them, not to please the equally flourishing snobs. He is at his comedic best when he treats satirically the many humorous aspects of the new acquisitive society (for modern capitalism was born in the Renaissance, first in Italy). The Jonsonian businessman, like our own today, is always busy trying to swing some clever deal to outsmart his competitors. But Jonson never romanticizes such businessmen (as Shakespeare comes dangerously near to doing with his money-lender, Shylock, or as Christopher Marlowe almost does with his usurer, Barabas, in *The Rich Jew of Malta*, before 1593).

Jonson's controlling idea seems to have been, like Moliere's, that in modern society men tend to run to extremes, and that social excess should be subjected to laughter. To these critically-minded comic writers, an excess of *anything*--even of virtue and wisdom--may become ridiculous. Thus, in *Every Man in His Humor*, the father, Knowell Sr., is no villain but honestly over-concerned lest his gay-spirited son, the hero Edward Knowell, may be going to the dogs amongst corrupt low companions in London. His excessive well-meant fatherly zeal starts the whole comic panorama of one day's imagined life into motion. In the end it turns out that young Ned Knowell was a perfectly decent chap all along, but a lover of practical jokes; and the merry, eccentric but sane Judge Clement, who straightens out all the comic confusions in the last act, cheerily advises the elder Knowell--laughing at *excessive* fatherly zeal: "What! your son is old enough to govern himself. Let him run his course; it's the only way to make a staid man...." (III.vii.102+; *Comedy*, p. 129).

Villains--what part have they in Jonson's comic vision of modern society? In this general view, this is our last major point of sharp difference between Shakespeare and Jonson. In both comedies and tragedies, Shakespeare imagined a whole gallery of villains, and indeed his romantic universe could not do without them. But the plain truth is, we suggest, that any halfway careful view of life-as-it-is shows us that there are no such things in everyday life as the stage villains. This comic-sinister type really belongs in melodrama more than anywhere else.

Ben Jonson, looking about him in the developing modern London society, found no villains. He did find rogues great and petty, cheats, frauds, con men and women, phonies, hypocrites--a lively spectrum of everyday forms of vice and folly. Such people appear often in his comedies, and they usually earn their comeuppance. Everyone of them has at least a touch of larceny in his soul, as some wag has said we all do. In short, Jonson essentially dispenses with the stage villain type altogether, since his controlling aim is to be honestly true to life. This, of course, never means what we know today as photographic realism, usually a crashing bore.

Every Man in His Humor: (1599)

Our suggestions can now be fairly terse since we have the basis of a general view of Jonson's comic vision to work from. With classical control of the dramatized element of time, Jonson succeeds, as few have done, in representing simply one whole day in the lives of his London characters. For everyone we meet in the comedy is such a person as we could have met in London around 1599. There are no exotic or far-fetched people, themes, or plot-elements. A consummate artist in his own terms, Jonson offers us the brilliantly-controlled effect of seeming naturalness. Everyone--the reader can work this out for his own entertainment--behaves just as he would, being the kind of everyday person we see him to be to start with. What happens in the imagined action can be readily summed up:

> An over-protective well-to-do father (Old Knowell) keeps his possibly vagrant or de-linquent son (young Knowell) under observation. A very conventional-minded businessman and husband (Kitely), fearful without cause for his young wife's marital fidelity, jealously watches her every move. Detecting old Know-ell's prying, young Knowell's resourceful servant (Brainworm) looks after his young master's interests and also "bears an active and ingenious part" in the whole action, de-lighting in making fools of anyone he can. Bright-spirited and young (in their twenties?) people (Knowell, Wellbred, Mistress Kitely, who is sister to Wellbred and Downright, and Bridgett [the merchant Kitely's sister who lives in his house]) entertain themselves by ironically encouraging a town gull (Matthew) and a country gull (Stephen) to make public

fools of themselves, each in his own
special way.

A swaggering phony soldier (the
splendid comic invention that is 'Captain'
Bobadil) "cudgels whom he can and accepts
a drubbing when he must," namely from the
really tough and very English type, Squire
Downright, who is contemptuous of supposed men-of-fashion and will take insults
and nonsense from nobody. Downright, a
"plain squire" or country-gentleman, constantly lives up to his name. And in the
end a jolly, crusty but kindly magistrate
(Justice Clement) uses all his legal auth-
ority--and some humorous Jonsonian exten-
sions of it--to see that every fool and
every reasonably sensible character in the
play gets his just deserts. (adapted from
John Palmer, *Ben Jonson*, p. 26.)

The whole artistry of this kind of plot-invention
is precisely that it beautifully allows the characters
to unfold before our eyes with a life-like seeming
naturalness and with a high degree of dramatic economy.

The alert reader may have noticed how little em-
phasis we have placed on the famous four 'humours' and
on Jonson's treatment of them. Tedious pages in many
literary histories belabor the subject. We think it
more useful to see that to Jonson's comic vision an
excess of *anything* becomes fair game for ridicule and
laughter which hopefully will clear the air of nonsense
and restore both the characters in the play, and the
audience which to some degree shares in their follies,
all to a better and more balanced frame of mind.

Actually Jonson's staged view of human psychology
makes quite good sense. It represents but one of the
Elizabethan concepts of human motivation. The droll
way of naming some of the characters at once gives the

audience a clue to some dominant character-trait, often
enough a trait which in him tends to become excessive
and therefore matter for fun-making at his expense.
Old Knowell tends to think he knows more than he does,
that he is wiser than events prove him to be. Brain-
worm lives up to his name and shows himself to be a
witty, merry knave and inventor of intrigues. George
Downright is a plain, down-to-earth, blunt or 'downright' man, very direct in speech and action. In contrast, Downright's half-brother is named Wellbred; he
is a gay young sophisticated man-about-town. The minor
character, Thomas Cash, earns his living as the merchant
Kitely's cashier.

But what is most intriguing and amusing about Jonson's view of character, his comic vision focused on the
normal human tendency to go to extremes at times, is
best seen in what may be called his comedy of *over-
reaching*. Before Jonson, Christopher Marlowe had invented the tragic over-reacher, the idea of a tragic
hero who may be eventually destroyed through the working out of the very qualities of heroic genius for
which is most outstanding and even admirable, as with
Marlowe's figures of Tamburlaine or Dr. Faustus, to
whom we shall return later in this study.

Jonsonian comedy, as in *Every Man in His Humor* and
The Alchemist, builds a sort of comic tower (as children delight to do with blocks)--higher, higher, more
and more precarious, until in the 4th and 5th acts the
whole thing has to collapse in laughter as all the chief
characters over-reach themselves, their major follies
come home to roost, and they themselves bring tumbling
down on their collective heads the comic tower they have
unwittingly built.

*Suggested Reading
(criticism of Jonson and his plays):*

Bamborough, J. B. *Ben Jonson*. New York, 1959.

*Barish, Jonas (ed.). *Ben Jonson: A Collection of Critical Essays.* Prentice-Hall, 1963 (paperback).

Barish, J. A. *Ben Jonson and the Language of Prose Comedy.* Harvard, 1960.

Chute, Marchette. *Ben Jonson of Westminster.* Dutton, 1953. (Lively, popular biography.)

Dessen, Alan C. *Jonson's Moral Comedy* (Northwestern University Press, 1972).

Enck, John J. *Jonson and the Comic Truth.* U. of Wisconsin, 1957.

Knoll, Robert. *Ben Jonson's Plays: An Introduction.* Nebraska, 1964.

Knowlton, Edgar. "The Plots of Ben Jonson," *Modern Language Notes.* XLIV, 1929, pp. 77-86.

Palmer, John. *Ben Jonson.* Viking, 1934. (Readable; inhibited by his persistence in measuring Jonson by Shakespeare.)

Partridge, Edward. *The Broken Compass: A Study of the Major Comedies of Ben Jonson.* Chatto & Windus, 1958.

Symonds, John. *Ben Jonson.* London, 1886.

Thayer, C. G. *Ben Jonson: Studies in the Plays.* Oklahoma, 1963.

IV   Laughing Chivalric Romance to Death:

Francis Beaumont's
The Knight of the Burning Pestle (1607)

    It is noteworthy that the played-out and done-for
stuff of the medieval chivalric romances was being
laughed to death in many parts of Europe almost at the
same time late in the Renaissance. In England, as early
as the More-Erasmus New Humanist group (*ca.* 1500-1535),
such romances, including the *Morte D'Arthur*, were satirized as asinine, as insults to the intelligence of even
fairly reasonable and well-informed men and women. By
the 1590's in England, satiric treatment of the sort of
un-lifelike absurdities often found in the old romances
(and myths) was fairly common. After such absurdities
of thought, feeling, and behavior have once been seen
to be just that, it is hard ever again to take them
seriously. Thus a Christopher Marlowe could write the
exquisite little narrative poem on "Hero and Leander"
(by 1593), retelling a fairly straight version of a
minor Greek romantic legend related to the antique world
of Greek mythology.

    But by mid-1597 that roistering Londoner, Thomas
Nashe, burlesques the old romance delightfully in
"Nashes Lenten Stuffe, or the Praise of the Red Herring,"
which includes 'Hero and Leander, or How the Herring
Became a Fish.' The once-pathetic and heroic climax of
Marlowe's version, when Hero discovers the drowned
Leander, is burlesqued thus:

    [First he must drown; or in Nash's words:]
    . . . the churlish frampold waves gave him
    his belly full of fishbroth, ere out of
    their laundry or wash-house they would

47

> grant him his coquet [exit-permit]; . . .
> and tossed his dead carcass, well bathed
> or parboiled, to the sandy threshhold of
> his leman [lover] for a . . . morning
> breakfast.
>
> [The 'romantic' tragic discovery]: Down
> (Hero) ran in her loose nightgown, and
> her hair about her ears, . . . and thought
> to have kissed his dead corse alive again,
> but as on his blue jellied sturgeon lips
> she was about to clap one of those warm
> plasters, boistrous woolpacks of ridged
> tides came rolling in, and raught [reached]
> him from her. . . . And that she . . . made
> no more bones but sprang after him, and so
> resigned up her Priesthood, and left work
> for Musaeus and Kit Marlowe.

After such satirists as Nashe had done their merry
work of exploding some forms of traditionally respectable literary nonsense, only the very old-
fashioned or naive could still take such supposedly
heroic and romantic doings seriously. There is
really no need to think that Francis Beaumont had
to have read Cervantes' grandly mock-heroic anti-
romance *Don Quixote* (published in Spanish by 1605;
the first English translation, Shelton's, was done
by early 1611, and printed in 1612 with a preface
claiming it was done five or six years earlier). Anyway, the delightful mock-heroic burlesquing of medieval romance that appears in *The Knight of the Burning Pestle* (probably written by 1607) becomes one element of the vigorously rising comedy of London life.

If a comparable play were to be written today in
the U. S. A., of course, targets of the burlesque
would include some combination of Soap Opera and The
Western,since in these two durably popular forms persist the perennial middle-class love of romance,how-
ever corny, improbable,absurd, or even downright bogus

treatment of human nature and the workings of society.
Indeed it might be argued that many forms of what come
gradually to be part of the literary or artistic
'establishment,' part, that is, of what the unthinking
accept naively at seeming face value, as conventional
wisdom of the day, is fair game for mock-heroic burlesque and satire. The resulting laughter, if fairly
critical, may clear the air of accumulated nonsense.
What really *was* valuable human truth in the subject
thus satirized will, we hope, survive in a healthier,
saner form to benefit us all.

We suggest that full enjoyment of such an uproar-
ious and rowdy play as *The Knight of the Burning Pestle,*
with its dominantly mock-heroic and anti-romantic satiric tone, requires that the audience or reader be consciously aware of the foolishness which is made fun of.
Pestle has three main elements, drolly intertwined.
Indeed we have two plays-within-plays, with one storyline now and then ludicrously and abruptly abandoned
in favor of another. *Pestle* may well be the first
'audience participation' comedy in English, for the
Grocer and his Wife provide the third element in the
comic brew.

As the play seems about to begin, a professional
actor labelled "Prologue" (a device by then already
stale) strikes a pompous stance and announces that his
company aims to present a play centered on London life,
"The London Merchant." Sensing rank ridicule of honest
tradesmen to be coming, a London businessman (the
Citizen, a wealthy grocer, rudely mounts the stage,
soon followed by his Wife, who has never seen any play
before), interrupts the actor, and angrily denounces
any and all stage-mockery of decent and, what is more,
wealthy merchants like himself! The actor with comic
abruptness drops the pretence that he *is* an actor.
(This sort of thing laughably throws away the entire
illusion that what the stage presents, the audience
should interpret as 'real.')

Thus the actor now speaks as everyday man-to-man, asks the grocer why he interrupts the show, and protests that the actors are unprepared to stage anything but the announced "London Merchant." But the grocer and his wife, who may not know much about the theatre but very definitely know what they like and will pay for, demand an entirely different sort of play. Indeed the grocer wants to see a play which has not even been written yet! To the actor's protests that no one can possibly stage such a non-play, the grocer has ready answers which make perfectly fine sense to him and to his 'romantic' tastes.

The grocer and his wife, their minds confusedly full of 'romance' (more than a little resembling *Don Quixote*), insist that they will order up their own play as they go along. The wife has her heart initially set on just one thing: she wants to see a stage-lion killed with a club or pestle (p. 208). And she is so fond of the grocer's workaday boy-apprentice, Ralph (or Rafe), declared to be a fine amateur actor himself, that she insists Ralph shall play the lead role in what becomes, by fits and starts, the wonderfully absurd play-within-the-play, or the story of the knight of the burning pestle. When Ralph, a sheepish lout of a fellow, also comes out of the audience and gets up on the stage, he is asked for a sample of his dramatic talent and obliges with a "huffing part"--an asininely brayed out parody of the heroic Hotspur's famous speech on honor (*Pestle*, p. 208; *I Henry IV*, I.iii.201+).

An obvious inference for us is that, within ten years after the nobly 'heroic' Hotspur was brought on stage by Shakespeare, such heroics had come to seem pretentious, inflated, and somewhat ridiculous to London sophisticates at least. But Ralph's bellowing hugely delights the Grocer and his Wife. The professional actor of the Prologue has by this point become a little desperate at the way things are getting beyond his control. To placate the Grocer, he gives way and says Ralph shall have some sort of costume if he will

50

just 'go in' (get out of sight). It is also clear to
the Prologue-actor that the Grocer is perfectly willing and able to *pay* well for what he wants: why not
humor him? (If you can't lick 'em, join 'em?) The
Grocer is all for titling his to-be improvised play
"The Grocer's Honor," but gladly accepts (without
sensing the Prologue-actor's ironic mockery of him) as
a substitute title, "The Knight of the Burning Pestle."

By line 124 of the 'Induction' (*Comedy*, p. 209),
order has been restored, as the Grocer and his wife
take chairs on the stage itself along with various
gentry who, as was in fact then customary, have paid
for these choice seats. One more minor crisis arises
when the Grocer, who has in mind for Ralph a "stately
part" although we see he does not know what it will be,
insists on stately music, for which he demands "shawms"
(a sort of oboe). The professional actors have none,
but the Grocer pays to have them quickly hired (probably from a nearby tavern?).

Thus order is restored, and the professional actor,
with double ridiculousness, now resumes the identical
stagily pompous stance and falsely poetic tone with
which he first began, and speaks the seven banal lines
(Introduction, ll. 147-153) he had already memorized.
Then, dropping right back to ordinary conversational
tones, he flatly warns the Grocer: "Thus much for what
we (professional actors) do; but for Ralph's part you
must answer for yourself." The Citizen-Grocer and his
wife are not a bit worried. They are sure that when
their demands are combined with Ralph's dramatic talents, the result will be smashingly successful! So
ends the Induction.

By now it should be clear to the audience that
we are going to get at least two plays for the price
of one. If the Grocer and his wife will permit, the
professional actors-as-such (for of course everyone
who takes a part in the whole show is actually a professional; only some pretend not to be, like the

Grocer, his Wife, or Ralph and his cohorts) will do
"The London Merchant." This turns out to be a wild
parody of a romantic love story centered on a clever
rascal of a poor apprentice who loves his rich master's
daughter. The second play is to be "The Knight of the
Burning Pestle," and this gradually turns into a riot-
ously foolish burlesque of chivalric romance in which
Ralph performs what the silly Grocer and his wife, who
make up its plot as things go along, fancy to be brave,
noble, and heroic deeds.

By the end of the Induction, moreover, it is clear
to us (the readers or audience) that first, the Grocer
and his wife may be expected to interrupt the dramatic
proceedings and comment on them whenever they feel like
it. Secondly, that these sturdily middle-class folk,
equipped with all the prejudices of their London business set, are so marvelously and comically naive as to
believe, without irony, that everything done on stage
is somehow utterly real, instead of what, of course,
it all is--simply make-believe!

Of course one inevitable and delightful result is
that the Grocer and his Wife get the plots and characters of "The London Merchant" hopelessly inter-mixed
with those of "The Knight of the Burning Pestle."

For the most part, the characters in "Merchant"
speak in a phony and stilted style which itself is a
deadpan parody of the language of worn-out stage
romances. That Ralph and his apprentice-aids are
bound for trouble soon appears. By Act I, scene iii
we see Ralph reading with passionate interest from a
silly romance. Not entirely a jackass, even Ralph has
the sense to be aware that there is, nowadays, a sad
discrepancy between the ways people behave in literary
romance as compared with their everyday actions in
Elizabethan London. [Maybe the fabled age of chivalry
is dead? if it ever existed?] Ralph says dolefully:

There are no such courteous and fair,
well-spoken knights in this age [= the
year 1607]: they [actual Londoners] will

52

call one "the son of a whore" that
Palmerin of England [a 'literary' char-
acter] would have called "fair sir;"
and one that Rosicleer [also 'literary']
would have call'd "right beauteous
damsel" they will call "damn'd bitch."

(I.iii.40+)

Which accurate observation prompts the Grocer's wife
to interrupt and speak directly across the theoretically unbridgeable if invisible gap supposed to separate the stage make-believe from the everyday world:

Wife. [Angrily reminiscent] I'll
be sworn will they, Ralph; they have
call'd me so a hundred times about a
scurvy pipe of tobacco. (I.iii.47-49)

(Historically, tobacco-smoking had begun barely a dozen
years earlier, and the good Grocer's wife finds it a
disgusting masculine habit: "Fie, this stinking tobacco [being smoked by gentlemen in on-stage seats near
hers] kills [me]!" [I.ii.141].)

The main actions in the "London Merchant" side of
the whole show form a pleasantly varied and implicitly
satiric excursion into the realms of the foolishly sentimental in comedy. The plot-contortions and teapot-
tempests are almost soap opera-like. Most of the
characters are expertly designed by Beaumont as burlesques of popular stereotypes, although there is one
brilliant exception, Old Charles Merrythought, some of
whose eccentric vigor has rubbed off on his scapegrace
favorite son, Jasper. Indeed the rigorous and highly
unlifelike *predictability* of the stock characters and
plot-elements in "London Merchant" are themselves part
of what we, the alert audience or readers, are tacitly
invited to laugh at.

Thus it is a comic certainty that the rich merchant Venturewell will have not an ugly but a beautiful

Doris Day-simple daughter (Luce). It is certain he
will stuffily insist that Luce marry a rich oaf
(Humphrey), and equally certain that the poor but
spirited apprentice, Jasper, will be fired from his
job for having the audacity to fall in love with Luce.
It is a certainty that the romantic-minded Luce will
go all out for the equally 'romantic' Jasper's dim-
witted plan to elope, without either financial resources or friends, or any fixed objective. It is no
less comically certain that the oafish suitor, Humphrey, will reliably make an ever-greater ass of himself,
missing no opportunities to this end.

   As for the true-lovers' adventures, Beaumont
varies them drolly. With a satiric reminiscence of
Shakespeare's addle-pated lovers, who take themselves
so seriously in *Midsummer Night's Dream*, Beaumont, by
his third act, even has Luce and Jasper lose their way
and wander all night in Waltham Forest, practically in
the London suburbs. It is there that we may roar with
laughter, or smile, when Jasper crazily comes up with
his 'romantic' test for Luce's love and devotion, by
the device of suddenly pretending he is about to kill
her. At this action, the Grocer's Wife, who without
irony takes all this absurd stuff to be real, is horrified and clamors to have the London cops summoned
from the Ludgate police post outside the theatre.

   Naturally we (experienced readers or playgoers,
or students of American soap opera and situation comedy)
are not in the least shaken up by all these on-stage
doings in the plot of "London Merchant." For we know
it to be dead sure that Jasper and his lovely Luce will
outfox her father and escape all harm, since it is an
absolute law in such romantic comedy that whatever is
labelled "true love" always wins out in the end (and on
time, too--including the commercials). The only question
is: by what device, no matter how far-fetched, will
these sappy lovers win? But who would be so heartless
as to withhold laughter from Jasper's ingenious coffin-
trick, which he springs on us by the end of Act IV
(pp. 236-237)?

In *Pestle*, the other main story line of course
follows the would-be heroic, chivalrous, honorable,
noble, glorious, patriotic and epic stage-exploits
which the Grocer's apprentice Ralph either invents,
stumbles into, or is ordered to perform by the Grocer
and his Wife, from their on-stage seats. Certainly
no teen-ager in all human history could be more willing to please than our Ralphie. Whatever any would-be
romantic and chivalric knight ever dreamed of doing,
Ralph will bust a gut trying to do better--for the
everlasting glory of all grocers (I.iii)! Obviously,
as he studies his absurd role in I.iii, he must become
--so says the book of romances he reads as a Bible--a
"courteous and well-spoken knight." Naturally for
such a paragon there can be only one possible career,
namely in greatly daring "feats" of arms, battling
giants, rescuing any and all "fair damsels" found in
distress! Two junior grocer's helpers, Tim and little
George, get into the loony action as Ralph's "trusty
Squire" [cp. Sancho Panza] and "Dwarf." So by the end
of I.iii (pp. 212-214), off goes this fearsome three-
some to search for glory. Ralph staggers along bearing
a shield, somewhat larger than he is, on which he has
emblazoned a burning pestle, in remembrance of his
former humble trade in the London grocery.

Even the romantically crazed Don Quixote never
had, in so short space or time, more absurd adventures
than our English Ralph and his fierce little "Squire"
and "Dwarf." In Waltham Forest, to the boys' astonish-
ment, *they* are mistaken for giants, while their first
would-be chivalrous efforts to relieve poor lost
gentlewomen go haywire (II.i; pp. 217-218). This was
bad luck enough but worse speedily ensues. For the
honest Grocer and his Wife, outraged by the rascally
apprentice, Jasper (from the "London Merchant" plot),
demand that Ralph meet Jasper in a fight. Glumly, the
professional "Prologue"-actor protests that "Merchant"
has no such fight in its action; but this sensible ob-
jection only arouses the Grocer's high wrath and his

Plot me no plots! I'll ha' Rafe come
out [and fight to order]; [or] I'll make
your house too hot for you else.

(II.v.70; p. 220)

I.e., since he is paying the piper, he is jolly
well going to call the tune! The "Prologue"-actor
shrugs in ironic despair, and promptly the *two*
'romantic' heroes appear to do combat. But while both
Jasper and Ralph have read romances enough to unhinge
their weakish brains, Jasper, a touch more practical,
has somewhere along the line also learned how to fight
in good Elizabethan London street-brawl style. The
side-liners, the Wife and the Grocer, cheer their boy
with shouts of "Break's pate [head], Rafe, break's
pate!" But poor Ralph gets ignominiously clobbered
and perhaps ends up sitting there on stage, blubbering
a bit, looking reproachfully at the Wife. Baffled at
this unlooked-for defeat, the Wife is again all for
calling the cops. But her husband, the honest Grocer,
is more expert in the cockeyed ways of romances. He
senses foul play; Jasper won only because he was "enchanted"; but the Grocer will order for his boy a
magic ring, and Ralph shall beat him yet!

Act III of *Pestle* is a masterpiece of mock-heroic
funmaking. It brings our Ralphie through the most delightfully absurd and (to us, not of course to him) the
funniest 'romantic' adventures yet. It seems that while
the true-lovers,Jasper and Luce of the "London Merchant"
plot, got lost all night in Waltham Forest, the chivalric Knight of the Burning Pestle, with his trusty
"Squire" and "Dwarf," very sensibly found comfortable
shelter at a sort of Elizabethan Holiday Inn, specifically at the Bell Inn. Now of course in those won-
drously literary things known as chivalric and medieval
romances, no "courteous Knight" is ever obliged to pay
a hotel bill. But the Inn-keeper of the Bell is realistically straight out of London life; he demands his
twelve shillings; and he is toughly not going to take,

instead of hard cash, any of "courteous Knight"
Ralph's pretty, puffed-up romantic speeches instead
(III.ii.1-53). It very much looks like Ralph is going
to get his head broken once more. But with absolutely
delightful naivete, the honest Grocer intervenes to
save the day. Taking all this silly make-believe to
be real (he has never heard of stage-money?), he digs
in his own pocket, walks across and gets into the
action briefly, and with contempt, pays Ralph's hotel
bill! then proudly resumes his seat and role as spec-
tator.

Thus placated, the Host, sardonically amused at
being heroically titled "Sir Knight of the Bell," by
now takes Ralph to be some queer kind of would-be practical joker. Why not play a counter-joke on *him*? So,
getting more than even, the Host himself suggests what
becomes Ralph's second and finest adventure. This is
the hugely farcical and mock-heroic confrontation with
the ugly, giant Barbaroso (really Nick, the village
barber, toothpuller, and surgeon), who dwells in his
"cave" (barbershop) nearby the Bell. The resulting
glorious adventures round out Act III of *The Knight of
the Burning Pestle*. As a whole, they surely add up to
Ralphie's finest hour, as a Sir Winston Churchill
might have said.

How much of such epic and chivalric glory can
flesh and blood stand? (Let alone the audience's sides,
which by now may be sore with laughter at so much of
the idiotic in romance piled artfully on what is pre-
posterous?) As Act IV begins, the Grocer and his Wife
are becoming sated and bored. Moreover, their inventive talents are just about exhausted. What shall
Ralphie do next? The Grocer's only idea is so stale
that even he drops it when told that another London
theatre, the Red Bull, has already done it (IV.i.50).
To aid reflection while racking his wits, the good
Grocer orders beer served to his sweating Wife and to
all the gentlemanly-spectators sitting with them on
the stage (p. 232). And a boy, in true Elizabethan

style, dances a jig, although his talents do not reach
to turning flip-flops or eating fire (IV.i.1-15).

The Grocer has just about run out of ideas, when
his Wife comes up with a 'romantic' scheme of which
(as Holzknecht said) "Hollywood might be proud." The
resulting splendidly absurd bit of romance is promptly
acted out by Ralphie & Co., who must be read and imagined to be laughed at (IV.i.52-62; p. 233). Beyond
this, it would seem impossible to go with mock-heroic
antics. Thus, after this one last creative outburst
of the Wife's is staged for her, the Grocer and his
Wife finally lose all interest in knight-errantry.
Being energetic Londoners and proud of it, they now
have a surge of civic pride. So, for the glory of all
grocers and for want of any other adventures to do,
Ralphie appears to order as Lord of the May, "with all
his scarfs about him, and his feathers, and his rings,
and his knacks" (IV.vi., pp. 238-239), and proudly
delivers an inflated specimen of asinine pseudo-poetic
speech such as Americans once knew as Fourth-of-July
oratory.

Then the good Grocer's civic pride gives way to
his everyday Londoner's delight in a lively and harmless military parade, which the docile Ralphie, now
turned heroic commander, sternly leads, every inch the
soldier (V.ii., pp. 240-241). The effect is a smashing
success which prompts the Grocer and his Wife to predict a great real army career for their beardless apprentice.

Like all good things, even Ralphie's grandly foolish and mock-heroic adventures must have their end.
Tear-jerking and pathos are now in order. Ralph must
die. He does, mock-superbly. Onto the stage he staggers, with a stage-prop forked arrow seemingly clean
through his head, ketchup running down his woebegone
cheeks. But since all this is 'romance,' not to be
confused with what we all know of everyday life,
Ralphie can and does take his sweet time dying. He

gives, in his best silly-epic style, a summary of his adventures and virtues, bids his soul "fly, fly . . . to Grocers' Hall," and "dies" smiling.

Then, of course, he instantly and cheerfully bounds up to bow and receive applause, then walks off stage, his job well done (V.iv.1-55; pp. 243-244). It is an artfully phony death-scene to end all unlifelike death-scenes on stage, including perhaps even some of those of which Shakespeare was so fond: in the last, the great hero, knowing he has a death wound, bleeds away but is nevertheless allowed to spout blank verse for 20-50 lines or so before relapsing into blessed silence.

Thus ends our brief sketch and critique of what happens in one of the most charming and ingenious of all London comedies, Francis Beaumont's *The Knight of the Burning Pestle*, first staged about 1607.

V   The Touch of Larceny in Every Modern Man

Ben Jonson's *The Alchemist*:   (1610)

Spencer (*Comedy*, p. 148) is right on target.   This
is "the most nearly perfect example" of Jonson's vigorous, realistic and satiric London comedy.   Diverse and
wide-ranging as is the panorama of characters eager to
be gulled by the three masters (Subtle, Face, and Doll
Common), each is quite individualized.   Yet the comic
speed of the action never slows down.   Rather, from the
first furious quarrel with which the comedy begins, and
which embodies the whole exposition of the controlling
plot-situation with such consummate ease,the comic pace
accelerates.

In the printed play (*Comedy*, p. 149), a droll sort
of anagram, "The Argument," sums up the entire action.
The play was written and first produced in a year when
the perennial plague was intense in London, and Jonson
makes rich use of London local color.   The plague, of
course, like many deadly epidemic diseases, raged worst
during the hot summer months.   Thus a well-to-do Black-
friars district householder, Mr. Lovewit, has left his
town house and, for his health, gone to live in his
country place, with its hopfields, until the epidemic
ends.   His return sooner or later is of course anticipated.   His butler, Jeremy (alias "Face" in the comedy)
has been left in charge of the town-house, which of
course has what is known as a 'respectable' address.

Time hangs heavy on Jeremy's hands, and he feels
certain his master will not return to London as long
as the plague kills even one a week.   While killing
time on the fringes of the London underworld it seems,
Jeremy has come to know a professional cheater or con
man, Subtle, and Subtle's punk of the moment, Doll

60

Common. This precious pair has fallen on lean days,
but the three rascals lay their heads together to
make the best of the opportunity they see to get-rich-
quick by gulling avaricious Londoners. The butler
Jeremy lends them his master's town-house and provides
the equipment needed for an alchemical laboratory,
which Subtle, a man of many talents, will operate as
'Doctor Subtle,' a supposedly pious and learned scientific researcher and one so devoted to pure knowledge as to be indifferent to money. Jeremy assumes
a new disguise, as 'Face,' the runner who prowls London for likely suckers and potential victims. He also
doubles as 'Lungs' to blow the bellows under the 'laboratory' fires. Doll Common, an attractive specimen
of the London streetwalking sorority, comes along and
occasionally practices her old trade on the side. All
three, then, will share in the take, as Jeremy/Face
and Subtle also share Doll as "their republic."

We begin the play when these talented rascals
have thoroughly ripened for the cheating a fine variety of clients, every one of whom, of course, quali-
fies as a victim and for our laughter exactly because
he has a touch or more of larceny in his heart. A
major killing is in prospect for Face, Subtle, and
Doll, if all goes well. They have been doing a roar-
ing business thus far. Their patrons including, we
hear, ladies and gentlemen, citizen's wives, knights
who drive up in coaches, assorted gallants, oyster-
women, sailor's wives, etc.; and even some strait-
laced Puritans of Amsterdam. These assorted suckers
come for horoscopes, or to be provided with invisible
'familiar spirits,' while the most ambitious hope for
the fabled "philosopher's stone" itself so as to get
rich by transmuting iron, etc. into legal gold. And
of course some are drawn by the lure of flat bawdry
with Doll Common, who is not above keeping up her old
business now and then.

Indeed, business has been so successful that, as
the play opens, the cheaters Face and Subtle furiously
insult and accuse each other of cunningly taking more

than his fair share of the take. Doll Common, more
practical than either of the men, desperately appeals
for peace, and this is sealed just as the first of the
day's suckers appears to be fleeced.

The fast and often rowdily farcical action which
follows provides the reader-spectator with an enter-
taining and adroitly varied panorama of London gulli-
bles. Dapper (Act I+), a too-smart young lawyer's
clerk, wants a 'familiar spirit' to pick winners for
him in raffles, horse-racing, and gambling. 'Doctor'
Subtle pretends such piety and affects such lofty
ethics that Dapper's gold is taken but with extreme
seeming reluctance.

Then Subtle reveals to the flattered Dapper that
he is allied to the Queen of Fairy. How can he lose
after this? He returns later in the day (III.iv.pp.
176+), is gagged with gingerbread, stuffed in the
privy, and naturally stripped clean of all the gold he
has on him! The second sucker to appear is one Abel
Drugger (Act I), a simple-minded tobacco-seller who
wants necromantic tips on the most profitable way to
arrange his store. Relieved before he goes of what
little gold he has, he departs flattered into believing, this callow youth! that he will be an Alderman
of the great London City by spring!

But these are small fry on which the delightfully
clever operators of multiple swindles have just been
warming up, as it were. By the end of Act I, they spy
really big game coming, no less than the wealthy Sir
Epicure Mammon, a mock-epic figure of insatiable greed.
And it is this very day on which 'Doctor' Subtle has
promised to complete the complex alchemical process by
which the "philosopher's stone" is made. (Of course
by now Sir Epicure has already been milked of a great
deal of gold, which it is understood has to be fed
into the laboratory apparatus before the stone can be
completed.) But why should Sir Epicure grudge his
already-large investment when he is utterly certain

that shortly he will be master of infinite wealth and almost magical powers, so that a return from puffing middle-age to fresh youth and Herculean sexual vigor will be his, at will? (For Mammon's appearances, Face quickly changes into his disguise as the amiable laboratory helper, Lungs.)

To be sure, Mammon is a rank hypocrite! as at II.iii.52+, where he blandly lies to Doctor Subtle (who is not fooled), that he only wants wealth "for pious uses,/Founding of Colleges and grammar-schools, /Marrying young virgins [i.e., by presenting them with free dowries], building hospitals/And, now and then a church"!

The fourth prospect, who accompanies Sir Epicure Mammon, is the hard-headed skeptic, Pertinax Surly. Stubbornly suspicious as his name implies, he is on guard against all confidence games, regards alchemy as but a charming cheat, and the sight of Doll Common convinces him the place is a bawdy-house (II.iii.226+). He makes such difficulties that the rascals (angered by his mean spirits, too) contrive a fake message to get him out of the way, lest the gulling of Sir Epicure be damped down.

Surly, of course suspects the rogues to be what we (the audience) know they are; and in Act IV, in a fine low-comedy sequence, he returns disguised as a Spanish count who knows no word of English but desires to visit Doll. Since the rascals feel safe, while they smile flatteringly they heap insults upon him (to Surly's secret delight), telling him the truth, that he will be cozened, emptied, drawn dry, and milked before he leaves! Indeed Surly precipitates a dire crisis for the rogues late in Act IV, when all their dupes are assembled together, for Surly throws off his disguise and denounces Subtle, Face, and Doll. The rogues rally their powers,call upon the fanatically Puritan brethren, who hate the Catholic Spanish, and Surly is thrown out.

To complicate the doings, Jonson even introduces as satiric targets two members of the then-rising extremist Puritan persuasion (in both politics and religion), Tribulation Wholesome and Ananias. These ostensibly pious men hope, when they get the philosopher's stone, to be able to bribe any powerful men who might, in church or state, oppose them. Tight-fisted, they refuse to part with gold until they see results; and Doctor Subtle ironically drives them away indignantly, as frauds (II.v. etc.)

Rounding out the lot of suckers are Kastrill and his sister, Dame Pliant. Kastrill, a rich young heir with a firm income of 3000 pounds a year, is eager to shine in London's circles of fashion, although truly he knows nothing of good manners and is prone to quarrel with everyone, thinking this to be required of a gallant. The swindle-operators see him as a rich potential prize. Dame Pliant, the only decent woman in the comedy, is a "rich, young widow....nineteen at the most...soft and buxom...a delicate dabchick." Compared to the worldly-wise Doll, the widow is a "good dull innocent"; but her brother Kastrill, having heard that Doctor Subtle is a skilled matchmaker, hopes to arrange a rich marriage for her.

In the end, of course, with comic predictability, the rightful owner of the house, Lovewit, returns. All the swindles by Subtle, Face, and Doll collapse at once, as the alchemical laboratory blows up. Subtle and Doll disappear over the fence, no doubt to try their nefarious skills elsewhere. And Lovewit, who delights in an intricate joke, gets the truth from his butler Jeremy (alias Face), forgives him, appropriates the loot in the house as now his property, and genially if unromantically marries Dame Pliant himself.

Thus, too simply, we see what happens in Jonson's *The Alchemist*.

VI   An Induction to English Renaissance Tragedy:

Persistent Aspects of the English Tragic Spirit

For Renaissance tragedy exclusive of Shakespeare,
I suggest you use an approach parallel to that recommended for comedy (See 'An Induction to English Renaissance Comedy'). Make an effort to disengage your mind
from assumptions and preconceptions derived from Shakespearean tragedy, however relevant to that wonderful
world of imagined human experience. Before Shakespeare
wrote a line for the stage, there were at least two
brilliant poets of the Renaissance tragic theatre,
Thomas Kyd of *The Spanish Tragedy* (*ca.* 1585), and the
hard-writing, hard-living genius of Christopher Marlowe
who, in his brief span of creative life (*ca.* 1586-1593)
tremendously enlarged the scope and perhaps radically
altered the nature of English tragedy, with such seminal
plays as *Tamburlaine, The Rich Jew of Malta, Edward II,*
and *Doctor Faustus*. Indeed Shakespeare himself, like
most other Renaissance playwrights, is deeply indebted
to Kyd and Marlowe.

———————————

Some Suggestions for Reading:

In *Tragedy*: Background and Source Materials (pp.
251-292), including the early 15th-century morality
play, *Everyman* (pp. 251-264); the material on the falls-
of-princes (or *'De casibus'*) tradition from the early
Elizabethan *Mirror for Magistrates* (pp. 265-274); and
the material on one Renaissance idea of villainy, the
'Machiavellian' (pp. 275-292).

But before Kyd's *Spanish Tragedy* began the great explosion of talent that is the Elizabethan drama in its heyday (1585-1630s), there had long been Englishmen who pondered the great issues which are central to a tragic sense of life, regardless of the literary form used to express it. In the brief essay possible here, we can at least touch on some of these explorations by English minds which were attracted to the central questions with which all tragedy is concerned. Namely, why is there so much suffering, especially needless suffering, in the world? and what does it all mean both for those most directly affected and for the living survivors?

Over the centuries from the time of *Beowulf* to the late Renaissance in England, many men had pondered on suffering, evil, and death. Obviously all these same questions are dealt with by all religions. Perhaps inevitably, the religious and the secular inquiries into tragedy tended eventually to intertwine and finally even to compete for the attention of thoughtful mankind, as they often do today.

Here are a few of the haunting questions which come up again and again over the centuries: Are suffering and evil inescapable and ineradicable parts of life? What powers or potentialities in human nature can men, or at least 'great' men, develop to cope with suffering, evil and death? Are men of necessity the blind victims of mysterious universal powers designated by such terms as "Fate" or "Fortune"? If there are presumed to be superhuman or divine powers ruling the universe, what is their nature and plan for human life? and what is man's relation to these powers? (For example, in *King Lear*, when Gloucester is near his lowest point, he surmises that

As flies to wanton boys are we [men] to the gods,
They kill us for their sport.

(*King Lear*, IV.i.38-39)

Is truly heroic greatness and human dignity really possible, at least to some men? What forces in human nature or in the universe tend to create tragic conflicts, and even to *add* to the evil and suffering already in the world? These are but a few of the questions which appear to have been pondered during centuries of active wondering. We suggest that before the Elizabethan age, elements of a native English tragic tradition or convention (meaning what men generally agree on) had begun to take on durable life.

One caution concerning the following brief survey of the English tragic spirit as reflected in literature regardless of its form (i.e., not restricted to the form of drama). Our evidence is necessarily drawn from surviving work. But evidently much even of what once was written has not survived to our time (for example, none of Shakespeare's play manuscripts is known to exist; and the remarkable first epic in the language, the finely primitive *Beowulf*, exists in just one charred manuscript copy).

But I do not think it necessary to assume that men can learn from past experience only through written records. I surmise that when subjected to comparable experiences (say, to the perils of a great storm at sea; or to the willful destruction of loved ones; or to gross human outrage and tyranny), the victims may be quite capable of rediscovering for themselves what earlier men had perhaps already experienced and tried their best to write down for posterity.

In short, this brief survey of the English sense of the tragic is at best a skeleton outline. It is not meant to justify any idea of so-called evolution, let alone of literary and dramatic evolution which led to Shakespeare's tragedies. Furthermore, I do not think it wise to restrict this historic retrospect only to what modern critics regard as literary masterpieces, for sometimes seemingly primitive and unsophisticated art can tell much about human experience to those willing to bring to it the requisite sensitivity and the relevant interpretative skills.

A brooding but often tough-minded tragic spirit permeates much of what survives from the Old English or Anglo-Saxon centuries (roughly) from about 600 A. D. to the Norman conquest of 1066). Probably no living Elizabethan could have made out more than an occasional word of the language used for such short poems as "Seafarer," "The Wife's Lament," or "The Husband's Answer," let alone the solitary major poetic masterpiece of that ancient time, the essentially pagan but superficially Christianized epic, *Beowulf*. But even so early we can recognize elemental aspects of what later on recur as characteristically English tragic responses to universal human experiences.

Beowulf himself represents the first image of a possibly tragic hero in our literature. No superman, he stands out as embodying the finest, most-admired attributes of his primitive world. Therein what is at stake continually is survival itself. In the epic, we meet no one who seriously expects life to be easy. The moods of nature, on land or sea, are prevailingly hostile or indifferent to human survival. The gods seem coldly aloof.

Essentially, as a tragic hero, Beowulf represents the great man as fighter against very long or almost hopeless odds. The supreme joy of this hero we no longer even have a common word to express: it is 'battle-joy'. His supreme virtues are generosity, bravery in the face of danger and anti-human evil, and loyalty to those to whom loyalty is rightly due. It follows that the ultimate human degradation is embodied in the man who, in the heat of the strife, turns coward or disloyal, as do all but one of those who went with Beowulf into his final fight, with the sinister fire-dragon. One noble soldier, young Wiglaf, stood by his lord and chief. "Together they killed (the dragon), the kinsmen two, / A noble pair. So needs must do / Comrades in peril." (Spaeth tr.)

In *Beowulf*, simply to lose one's life is merely
to meet the inevitable doom of all men. To lose it by
wilful dishonorable action *is* tragic.

"The Wife's Lament," as the poem is now titled,
is brief and poignant. It is one of the few Old English poems whose imagined speaker is a woman. We learn
that her husband has been exiled overseas, for his
kinsmen plotted to "wedge apart" the lovers. She
weeps for his loss but is sure her faraway husband's
"Sharpest of sorrows...must suffer/Remembering always a
happier home." (Kennedy tr.) But the wife is no quit-
ter; she hangs onto hope with tenacity; and her spirit
expresses determination to keep human dignity in the
face of harsh degradations. The theme of tragic separation is echoed back in "The Husband's Message." In
this the dramatic 'speaker' is a wooden tablet on which
the exiled husband has carved a message to his wife, to
struggle for freedom, take ship and rejoin him. The
two wonderful little pieces may epitomize an elemental
idea of tragedy as a struggle for happiness against the
united forces of nature, fate, and evil men.

In none of these Old English poems does the poet
appear to have any respect for self-pity. The tragic
mood is rather dominated by a kind of grimly tough and
even, paradoxically, cheerful kind of basic stoicism
which celebrates, by understatement, qualities of credible human nature which may enable brave men and women
to survive with human dignity, if survival is possible
at all.

Centuries after the Old English world vanished or
went 'underground,'in the medieval English culture,
many more or less explicit ideas on tragedy flourished
in a curiously disorderly way. Such a powerful thinker
as a Thomas Aquinas might have felt a need to bring
harmony out of such confusion, but English medieval
critics and audiences apparently largely lacked such a
compulsion or talent.

Efforts have been made lately to define parts of Chaucer's imagined little universe of men as tragic. Specifically, his characterization of the Pardoner (*Canterbury Tales*) has been asserted to be so. Minor ecclesiastical functionaries, the official pardoners of the Middle Age were in effect licensed by the world-wide Roman Catholic church to receive confessions for sins and literally to sell pardons to those judged truly repentant. By Chaucer's time (*fl*. 1385-1400), such sales of pardons had often degenerated into a racket or pure fraud, which many good men denounced as a corruption before Martin Luther came along to do so. And Chaucer's Pardoner is a deliberate and very expert con man, who lugs about with him what he perfectly well knows are absolutely bogus holy relics and who peddles fake pardons to anyone gullible enough to pay him for them. Is not this wilful sinner a 'tragic' figure-- the only lost soul among the Canterbury pilgrims?--I reason, no.

For vicious and corrupt as he is, it is always theoretically possible, under Catholic doctrines, for the Pardoner himself, before he dies, truly to repent his manifold sins, via confession, so as to receive absolution, and to find the Catholic way to his soul's salvation. Hence the Pardoner figures in what has been rightly termed broadly the medieval "Comedy of Evil" (D. Cole, *Suffering and Evil in the Plays of Christopher Marlowe* [1962], Chap. I).

What of Chaucer's Monk's Prologue and Tale (*Canterbury Tales*), with its dreary compilation of brief histories of men who fell from high places or "degree" to low? Riches to rags, supreme power to powerlessness--one could go on and on. Indeed the Monk tediously does so, boring everyone beyond endurance, until the Knight courteously shuts him up. Partly the boredom was justified, for none of the characters whose lugubrious falls the Monk narrates come through as vivid personalities. All are cardboard outlines, and the 'falls' are mechanical in effect.

Underlying the Monk's brief stories, however, is one concept of tragedy that many medieval men, and some later, took seriously. It may be represented by the metaphor of the wheel of Fortune. To its imagined rim are bound all great or would-be great men. As the wheel revolves, driven by the mysterious, fitful impulses of chance, men may rise to the top; but certainly in due time they will be brought low, to misery and death. Moralizing with a heavy hand, the Monk delights in indicating that usually excessive pride went before the fall. As the "Falls-of-Princes" idea of tragedy, it had enough power to linger on into the late 16th century in England, as proved by the "Induction" to the *Mirror for Magistrates* (1559+; in *Tragedy*, ed. Ornstein-Spencer, pp. 265-274).

In our Introduction to English Renaissance Comedy we mentioned the *Second Shepherd's Play* as a fragment of the huge cycle-plays, broadly known as the liturgical drama because they originated in offshoots of the liturgy in the medieval Catholic churches. (An entire reconstructed cycle can be seen in *Specimens of the Pre-Shakespearean Drama*, ed. John Manly, Vol. I.) Taking these dramas as sweeping wholes, is the figure of Christ himself almost the archetype of a tragic hero? What about God's arch-rival, Satan? is he a tragic character (as some readers of Milton's late 17th-century *Paradise Lost* have thought him to be)? After the Fall, with the consequent expulsion from the Garden of Eden, are Adam and Eve to be regarded as elemental tragic figures? Does the entire story of mankind according to the Bible's account of human history, from its divine creative beginning to its future divine creative as well as destructive end at the Judgment Day, itself constitute the most tremendous and truly tragic drama possible for the minds of Christian men to conceive?

Without, I hope, in the least diminishing the moral grandeur, beauty and terror of this heroically-scaled vision of existence of earth, I would nevertheless conclude that these dramas were *not* tragic, either then or now, at least to firmly-believing Catholics such as presumably mostly made up 15th century audiences.

Actually the liturgical drama, at least from a 20th century viewpoint, appears to have been a peculiar "comedy of evil." As arch-villain, Satan and his devil-cohorts had, in the cycle-dramas, the role of subverting God's purposes for mankind. But the audience, as long as Catholic orthodoxy held firm, was certain that Satan was bound to fail. Hence his subversive efforts were hugely comic. And in historical fact, Satan's role became that of a great comedian, or comic villain, although of course played seriously.

But the liturgical drama did perhaps contribute one element of major enduring importance to the development of English tragic thought before the great Elizabethan drama appeared. For such drama implicitly required thoughtful spectators to rise above petty everyday concerns, to view the entire universe as permeated with a divinely ordained moral purpose, and to view all life on earth, and above all each individual human life, as of concern to both God and Satan, to the supreme powers of good and evil.

Of course, historically far antedating the medieval English drama, St. Augustine defined an answer to the haunting question, why is there so much misery in human life? And his answer implicitly is fused with most pre-Elizabethan thought on tragedy. His answer, put simply, was that human misery resulted from man's sinfulness, which God, through divine Providence, was duty-bound to punish. Whenever erring mankind would abandon sin, God would cease his just and wrathful punishments for disobedience to the divine will.

Of course some might say: why should the innocent suffer along with the guilty? For this, too, the classic theologians had a seemingly irrefutable answer—that all mankind was tainted by original sin, after the

Fall of Adam and Eve. By such reasoning, absolute innocence was impossible for mankind, although of course
not all were equally sinful. But the Fall was fortunate in one sense, for without it there would have been
no need for Christ to come upon earth to redeem man
from his otherwise dismal, hopeless state. (See
Herbert Weisinger, *The Fortunate Fall*.) Eventually,
at the Judgment Day, justice would be done, and there
would be a 'happy ending' (traditionally appropriate
to comedy) for those whose souls merited salvation,
while the damned would receive their proper punishment.

Does the morality play, such as the famous *Everyman* (*ca*. 1485; *Tragedy*, pp. 251-264) embody some genuine tragic vision and some idea of a credible tragic
hero, Everyman himself? I suggest, yes. The Messenger,
who speaks first, politely and gravely reminds the
audience what it already knows, that life is transitory
and death must come sometime. But then God appears as
a character and gives His view of the human condition.
God is deeply disappointed in what mankind has generally
made of the opportunities of life on earth.

In what follows (pp. 253-4), there are profound
consequences for the Renaissance and modern senses of
tragedy. Inherent in God's view of man, as we see it,
is the idea that man had been endowed with reason (like
the angels), but that there must or may be some terrible
flaw in human nature. Accordingly, instead of living by
reason, divine love and divine law, mankind generally,
compulsively or carelessly, gives way to base passions
and to their related vices and sins. But while careless
mankind, absorbed in everyday folly, sensuality, and
materialism, may have forgotten the eventual certainty
of divine justice, God has not.

Thus this assurance of divine justice becomes a
key element in the tragic vision here shown us. And
God concludes his reflections with an idea of tremendous
tragic import, namely, that only when man is forced to
face the imminent certainty of his own personal death,

is it possible for him to measure the meaning of his whole previous life. As a 'character,' God seems to speak more in sorrow than in wrath; he does not seem to be vindictive or malicious, does not seem prone to over-punish man for the mess he has made of himself.

In *Everyman*, therefore, there seems an underlying premise that man has free-will. Besides this, a central part of its tragic vision is the view of the human condition as almost inescapably involving a radical conflict between "reason" and "passion." Men use their power of free choice at their own peril; and it is highly ironic that they pursue everyday pleasure and profit, or happiness, all the while unknowingly getting ready for a dreadful day of reckoning with the reality of death and divine justice. And since death is personal, an inescapable part of being human, a possibly tragic part is an awful final loneliness.

As long as he fatuously tries to con God by thinking to evade His great agent, Death, Everyman is a fine target for satiric laughter, or, more precisely, for tragic and almost mock-heroic satire. Thus far we (the audience) may laugh heartily at him, unless, with an ironic shock, we stop to sense how much like most of us the character of Everyman really is. But the hero becomes a figure of at least intense pathos and of some belated heroic human dignity, when, cornered, he does confront the full horror of his predicament, then rallies all his modest powers to go to his own death. Only then, at long last, does he appear to be most fully conscious of the meaning *both* of his largely wasted life and of his imminent departure from life.

Does the central body of English medieval romance, the stories of King Arthur and his allegedly noble knights of the Round Table, contribute anything of importance to the growing English tragic sense of life? Widely popular as romances were among the upper classes in the Middle Ages, Sir Thomas Malory's huge compilation, the *Morte D'Arthur*, gained access to an ever-

74

growing and enthusiastic readership after its first
printing in 1485. Among its most glamourous figures
are those of King Arthur, his Queen-wife Guinevere,
and her traitorous lover, Launcelot. This triangle
is matched by that of King Mark, his Queen-wife
Isolde, and her traitorous lover Sir Tristram.

We think it likely that at least these two haunting stories of truly death-marked love did, in the
end, enlarge English tragedy, for many of the great
Elizabethan writers. But there were radical differences between romance's influence on Shakespeare and
his rivals, differences to be seen later on in such
plays as Kyd's *Spanish Tragedy*, Chapman's first *Bussy
D'Ambois*, Webster's *White Devil* and *Duchess of Malfi*,
Middleton-Rowley's *The Changeling*, and John Ford's
poignant *The Broken Heart*, to name but a few.

Several pattern-elements distinguish 'romantic
love' in these stories, of which that of Tristan and
Isolde is now the most famous, thanks to Wagner's
opera, with the despairingly beautiful but necessary
climax in the Liebestod, or love-death music. Malory
is incapable of saying why, but the great figures of
the world of the *Morte D'Arthur* may be seen moving,
almost inevitably, to their destruction and death,
all the while driven by passions and compulsions as
irresistible as beyond their powers of comprehension.

At the heart of such medieval romance lies a mystery, a fatal attraction, which may briefly be illustrated by the ruinous triangle formed by King Mark,
Isolde, and Sir Tristram. What they do frequently de-
fies common-sense. But as Denis de Rougemont (*Love
in the Western World*--highly recommended) shrewdly an-
alyzes the matter, the 'language of day' and life cannot clarify that of 'night' and death.

First of all, in these medieval romances, romantic
love, with its overwhelming mutual idealistic view of
the beloved as uniquely desirable, is always adulterous.

Secondly, as de Rougemont shows, with a wealth of examples ranging down to our own age, what such lovers
sub-consciously desire, beneath all veneers of reason,
is suffering and death. The forces that whirl them to
their doom are finally contemptuous of life itself.

In modern tragic literature, Tristan and Isolde
have become almost the archetypes of tragically romantic lovers. We however identify their relation as
death-marked, for with all its occasional beauty there
is about it something deeply morbid and sick. (In contrast, in our view, although Shakespeare uses for them
the *term* "death-marked," we regard his Romeo and Juliet
as life-marked--they are drawn as essentially healthy
people who want primarily to be left alone to enjoy
normal and Christian marriage.)

Only when we penetrate the masks can we see that
what such lovers as Tristan and Isolde, or probably
Shakespeare's Antony and Cleopatra, desire most is precisely the catastrophes and wide-spreading suffering
which they create. Sub-conscious forces, from our
modern viewpoint, form the ruling and underlying dynamic
of such romance. The lovers gradually lock themselves
into a vicious circle. Refusing to escape from it, and
ultimately contemptuous of life-forces, they deviously
seek and finally achieve a love-death. We may perhaps
be able to see that from *their* viewpoint, paradoxically,
this end is not merely a calamity but a cherished calamity. (In addition to de Rougemont, for those interested not only in such vicious circles but in possible
escape from them, we recommend Karl Menninger's *Love
Against Hate* [1942].)

The whole grand matter of such romantic love, when
regarded as an heroic and splendid destiny by the
lovers, is too intricate to be dealt with here in more
detail. The romantic-love complex, in variants including the Petrarchan, seems at once to have strongly attracted and strongly repelled many English Renaissance
tragic writers. (For the Petrarchan form, see J.

Lever's *The Elizabethan Love-Sonnet*.) They could
sense that far-reaching conflicts and resulting dis-
asters might well arise when the imperious demands of
such an heroically-scaled passion were set against the
laws and practical nature of existing societies. In
short, we suggest that the ideas of romantic love, as
they came to the late Elizabethans, enlarged their
sense of the suffering which could result when reason
and passion meet in head-on collision.

With the coming of the Renaissance to England,
around the beginning of the 16th century--soon followed
by the revolutionary tumults of the Reformation, as it
spread through Europe after the appearance of Martin
Luther--the forces confusedly blending to heighten the
English sense of tragedy become almost too complex to
be briefly set down. I can mention but a few of the
most notable, either in literature or in social history.

It is an untidy story. But this should surprise
no one, for the English, incurably eclectic, have again
and again fused in their culture elements which pure
logic would suggest to be irreconcilable. Even in the
late 20th century, they persist in keeping an heredi-
tary and aristocratic monarchy as the nominal frosting
on the cake of a more or less socialist-welfare state,
itself jostling along with the lively remains of 19th
century private-enterprise capitalism.

Some radical 'new' Renaissance ideas combined with
those drawn from contemplation of the historic fallen
grandeurs of ancient Greece and Rome, as 16th century
editors, translators, and printers busily brought out
almost the entire body of surviving ancient literature,
with perhaps one striking exception--the classic Greek
drama, which is highly lyrical and largely baffled the
translators' powers.

One radical idea, relevant to the tragic sense of
life, emerges from the More-Erasmus circle. More
clearly, perhaps, than any others of *ca.* 1500-1535,

77

they saw it to be possible for modern man to create
for himself on this earth, here and now, a 'good life.'
This represents a crucial break with the traditional
medieval view that this existence was miserable of
necessity and that true happiness could come only in
some after-life. But these humanists themselves lived
to see that, in their own time in England, at least,
those actually in power preferred war to peace, vain
dreams of ambitious chivalric conquest to the orderly,
peaceful reconstruction of English society.

Here we have genuine social tragedy, a tragedy of
human *waste*; and we suggest that most of the notable
tragedies written since then incorporate an idea of
tragic waste. (The story of this new-humanist search
for a good life may be found in Robert P. Adams' *The
Better Part of Valor* [1962].)

These new humanist ideals for a good life were
radical in another way, for their critique of man and
society pointed to an alternative to the Augustinian
explanation as to why there was so much suffering in
the world, the theologically traditional concept that
suffering arose because of mankind's persistent sinfulness and God's answering punishment via divine
Providence. If the new humanist idea made sense,
however, it meant that modern man was his own worst
enemy, for all but inescapable suffering (e.g., the
necessity of death) was man-made. Thus a whole new
heroic dimension was added to the tragic sense of
life and its possibilities.

In our comment upon *Everyman*, we noted the feeling of intense isolation and loneliness of the hero's
last moments of imagined life. Perhaps the very root
ideas of the Reformation eventually were bound to add
still another dimension to a much more acute loneliness as part of the modern tragic condition of man.
For the Reformation, in its various nationalistic
forms, essentially cut off Protestants from reliance
on the entire comforting structure of the Catholic

church, reaching from the humblest priest to the Pope himself, with his traditional infallibilities as God's deputy on earth. Rapidly the Protestants divided into sects, but each sect confronted the problem: on what authority are religious matters to be decided? (Bishops? Presbyters? etc.) But there is a potentially, and eventually in history a very real answer to this problem of ultimate authority. This is that perhaps every man not a firm practicing Catholic may have to deal directly, without intermediaries, with his wrathfully-just God.

One result is a tragic sense of utter loneliness and isolation, or alienation, as is more often said today. This sense, we think, may oddly enough be found in many of the tragedies. It appears when Kyd's Hieronimo (*Spanish Tragedy*) despairingly wonders whether the heavens are just, or whether he is without all aid in his search for justice. It appears in strange guise in the terrifying last act of Marlowe's *Doctor Faustus*, when Faustus feels sure he is cut off from God and that prayer is useless. It appears in the fifth-act torture scene in Chapman's first *Bussy D'Ambois*, when Montsurry proves incapable of "Christian reconciliation" with his estranged wife, Tamyra. It appears in the dreadful climax of Webster's *White Devil*, when the dying Brachiano can only scream "Vittoria! Vittoria!" And it takes other forms in *The Changeling* and *The Broken Heart*.

I suggest, therefore, that a vastly heightened and fearful kind of loneliness became, to Renaissance tragedians, part of the human condition which they felt bound to show. (In *King Lear*, as though to emphasize this despair and loneliness, Shakespeare invents a *pre*-Christian world, one in which very small comfort, if any, can be derived from the references to "the gods.")

The growing English tragic sense of life was further heightened by 16th-century reflections on human history. To the critically minded humanists, the vanished civilizations of Greece and, above all, of Rome represented

79

the mightiest cultural achievements of earlier Western mankind. Speculation on why Rome fell, and more broadly on comparisons of ancient and modern life, added a new dimension to tragedy. To some it seemed quite likely that new kinds of modern barbarism were quite capable of enhancing tyranny if not of destroying civilization.

"Good kings are a theoretical possibility but tyranny is an ever-present danger"--this was Sir Thomas More's favorite theme in his poems, which he dared not publish. More than any other European nation, the English, over the centuries from the Magna Charta onward, had developed a sense of freedom and human dignity under law. To many among such a people, the destruction of freedom and the rise of tyranny becomes part of the tragic sense of life. (Cf. the tragic satire on the plebeians at the outset of Shakespeare's *Julius Caesar*.)

From humanist reflections on western mankind's presumed earliest history there came, with renewed intensity in the 16th century, one of the most tragic possible secular views of human nature and its history, as well as of its present prospects. Earlier we noted the "comedy of evil" in the Christian view of human history, dramatized in the English Corpus Christi plays, tracing man from Creation to the Judgment Day, that is to the ultimate happy ending destined for the righteous. But classical antiquity provided a competitive account of the matter, embodied in the famous myth of the Golden, Silver, Bronze, and Iron Ages (Ovid's *Metamorphoses* gives the best-known version).

According to this story, man's first condition on earth was the best, and all history since the Golden Age is one of irreversible, progressive degeneracy. At the heart of the Four Ages progression is the idea that man has, in his deepest nature, some fatal flaw. Such a gloomily pessimistic view of course helped to answer the tragic question: why is there so much needless suffering in the world? Critical Renaissance pessimists, when they noticed scientific or technological developments, were apt at once to observe how swiftly such advances (e.g., gunpowder, metallurgy, the marine compass) were employed by vicious men for senseless destruction of their fellows in ever-widening wars. A humanist proverb, cited by Erasmus--"Man is wolf to man"--indicated that the human race itself may have a tragic destiny.

Countering this tragic pessimism, and increasing the tension and wonder about the fate of modern man, was an offsetting optimistic myth, that of Prometheus. The Prometheus myth represents man's earliest condition of life on earth as miserable in the extreme. "Nasty, brutish, and short," Hobbes was to say. Hope began when the Titan, Prometheus, defying the Olympian gods, taught our earliest ancestors how to use fire. From this came all later technology, and from technology (we are to believe) springs human happiness. This heroic myth, therefore, embodied a credible idea of man-made progress and could be used to justify an optimistic view of the human prospects.[1]

As late as *ca.* 1585-1640--the great period of the Elizabethan drama--few men could see any practical benefit from science, however, whereas the antihuman uses of technology in war were obvious. Sir Francis Bacon had few rivals in his vision of a human future made gloriously utopian through science and technology, but serious English optimism for his cause waited until after 1660 and the founding of the Royal Society. There is nothing anachronistic in Marlowe's representation of Dr. Faustus as a supreme scientist who gains universal knowledge by selling his soul to the devil,

---

[1]On the Golden Age and Prometheus myths, see: *The Better Part of Valor* (1962); A. Lovejoy & G. Boas, *Primitivism and Related Ideas in Antiquity* (1935); J. B. Bury, *The Idea of Progress* (1920).

fritters away his opportunities to use his science,
and only by seeming whim does not carry out his dreams
of vast destruction among mankind.

At least one major recent critic of the tragic
drama (Irving Ribner, in *Jacobean Tragedy*, 1962) argued shrewdly that tragic insights derived from contrasts of Golden age man with modern man lie at the
heart of the best work of Chapman, Tourneur, Webster,
Middleton, and Ford. He thinks (I believe, too simply)
that the tragedy of Chapman's *Bussy* (1600-1604) exemplifies the central problem of non-Shakespearean tragedy:
"(It) is the tragedy of all of us who must live in a
world where such virtues [as those of unfallen, golden-
age man] can no longer exist" (p. 7). The major thrust
of this main body of tragic drama is said to be based
upon the "assumption of a degenerate decaying world in
which virtue is incapable of survival." Hence the only
hope of the assorted tragic protagonists seems to be to
meet the "corroding force of the world's evil" with
some kind of stoicism, with some of its ideals of what
it is to be "a man." Professor Ribner found that all
these English artists, with individual variations, were
struggling "to find a basis for morality in a world in
which the traditional bases no longer seem to have
validity."

Further, he thought that the tragic pessimism of
these Jacobean tragedians links them to our own 20th-
century "age of anxiety." Opposing Chapman, Webster &
Co. in their own time, Ribner found to be the "conservatives" Shakespeare and Heywood. These two alone were
still able to show tragic protagonists sustained by
the "optimistic Christian humanism of the early Renaissance which stressed always the dignity of man and the
providence of God": so that accordingly their dramatic
imitation of the perpetual battle of man "against the
forces of evil in the world" leads to reaffirmation "of
order and design in the universe."

For thoughtful Elizabethans, scrutiny of great men
and their history certainly contributed to an increased

sense of tragic dread for their own time. Briefly,
we can cite three ways in which the literature shows
as much: (1) the 1563 poem, "The Induction" to the
famous *Mirror for Magistrates*; (2) Shakespeare's use
of historical sources; and (3) use of history by other
tragedians. Thomas Sackville's "Induction" (in *Tragedy*,
pp. 265-274), as the title-page of the whole work shows,
was hopefully designed to benefit great men in actual
places of decisive power and implicitly to induce them
to use their power for good rather than evil. Of course
above all the authors of *The Mirror* and its "Induction"
hoped to influence Queen Elizabeth herself. Underlying
the "Induction" is a basic humanistic assumption that
the critical study of the past, through history and
biography, is intensely relevant to the present. Implicitly, the poem suggests something of the much later-
defined idea that those who refuse to learn from history
are doomed to repeat it.

Sackville's handling of imagery to build the atmosphere of a wintry landscape, hideous with waste, ruin,
and death is strong. His very English insights, recall-
ing *Everyman*, show too in the singular way in which he
makes poetic abstractions seem vividly real to the sym-
pathetic reader. Peopling his landscape are grimly
horrid figures: Sorrow (11.71-175), Remorse of Conscience (1.219), Dread (1.232), and fell Revenge
(1.239+). Their fit companions are sheer Misery and
greedy Care (1.271) with his "cousin of Death, heavy
Sleep."

After them comes "sad Old Age" (11.295-336), a
sort of pre-image of Death itself. Close by are "pale
Malady...with breath corrupt" (1.337), then Famine
(1.344), and lastly great Death himself (1.372+), next
to the heroically-scaled figure of War (1.386+). War
bears a great shield, reminiscent of Achilles' in the
Iliad, and on it are portrayed the great men of antiquity who perished in battle. To the poet's eye, the
fall of Troy (shown on the shield) seems the climactic
metaphor of tragic suffering. Ferried over the river

Acheron, Sorrow arrives finally at the Kingdom of Hell itself (1.505), a melancholy place all peopled by the results of human folly of vast dimensions.

Then the reader meets (1.533) the first of the figures of great men who fell from high place, Henry, Duke of Buckingham. *This* Buckingham (1454-1483) was the arch-confederate of the tyrant, Richard III, and Shakespeare readers meet him in *Richard III*, where he is hustled to execution. But some 1563 readers may have had memories, too, of Edward Stafford, 3rd Duke of Buckingham, whose death in 1521 marked the beginning of Henry VIII's terrible series of "judicial murders" which stretched over a quarter-century and ended only with the tyrant-king's death.

Indeed, when Henry VIII's daughter Elizabeth became queen in 1557, many men expected a ferocious anti-Catholic series of executions to begin. When Queen Elizabeth refrained from such a policy, John Foxe (in prefaces to his famous *Book of Martyrs*, 1563 etc.) expressed a widely shared sense of thanks and wonder for her divinely guided clemency. In short, while the falls-of-princes ideas of tragedy has medieval roots, for Elizabethans it had urgent modern relevancy. To quote Sir Thomas More again, "Good kings are a theoretical possibility, but tyranny is an ever present danger."

It begins to seem that a major insight of English Christian humanist thought on history is that by and large the western world's history is itself partly a record of endless social tragedy. The fall of man from pre-historic innocence and peace appears both in the Biblical account of Eden and in the pagan Golden Age myth. But while the Christian view predicted a glorious ending for the righteous at the final Doomsday, until that event arrived the prospects for human happiness on earth seemed for misery as usual but with degeneracy and needless suffering very probably ever-increasing.

Reflections on the successive corruptions, from the Golden Age to the Iron Age and so to modern times intensified the idea that man has some fatal flaw, that man is his own worst enemy, and that human history is mainly a story of human suffering. No feature of known historic behavior seemed, when leading English humanists looked back on the past, more characteristically human than the increasing addiction to war, which ever tended to become more savage and total.

If and when a generation of great tragic writers should arise in England, as so surprisingly happened after Kyd's pioneering *Spanish Tragedy* (*ca.* 1585), would these artists be almost sure to turn to history, written and unwritten, as a prime source of tragic truth? It seems that they were and did, in many different ways.

Shakespeare, we observed, never represents that the action of his plays is supposed to be unmistakably in contemporary or near-contemporary England, or even very specifically in recent Europe. His two favorite sources, however, were historians: *Holinshed's Chronicles* (e.g., for many history plays, *Macbeth, King Lear)* and Plutarch's *Lives of the Noble Grecians and Romans* (tr. North, 1579). Yet Shakespeare's tragic vision is distinctively his own. He does not owe it to these sources. Rather he reworks his materials selectively, inventing at times, imposing his gradually developed tragic sense of life upon what he took to be historic fact.

But, unlike Shakespeare, other great Elizabethan tragic writers--e.g., Kyd, Marlowe, Chapman, and Webster--*did* find that nearly contemporary history provided intense stimulation to their tragic vision. We now know that the plot of *The Spanish Tragedy* was Kyd's invention, but it is represented on stage as a complex of events following the historic battle of Alcantara in the early 1580s. One of Marlowe's lesser plays, *The*

Massacre at Paris, centered, for a largely Protestant English audience, on the St. Bartholomew's Day (1572) mass-murder of Huguenots in Paris, led by the Catholic villain of the piece, the Duke of Guise. Chapman's remarkable first *Bussy D'Ambois* imaginatively adapts historic events at the almost contemporary French court of Henry IV; and the same hated Guise reappears, now playing second fiddle to a greater villain.

Webster's view of tragedy, to Victorians, seemed so lurid as to pass credibility. But the *Duchess of Malfi* draws directly on Italian history of 1510-1513; while *The White Devil* strongly re-tells, with understatement, a tragedy of real Italian life which had made a "deep impression in Italy a quarter of a century before," as F. L. Lucas noted. Thus some of the finest Renaissance writers found no need to go to the distant past or to fiction for complex stories calculated to show how modern man had become wolf to man.

Virtually all the great tragic writers, like most intelligent, literate Elizabethans, were deeply influenced by what they took to be Machiavellianism, regarded as a tremendous force for evil driving many great men in modern society. (See, in *Tragedy*, pp. 275-291, part of the translation of Gentillet's famous, widely-known attack, *Contre-Machiavel*.) Reliable editions or translations of Machiavelli's Prince (written by 1516) or other works were scarcely available in Elizabethan England. Rather the brilliant Florentine and his views of what happens in history acquired a sinister character and reputation through such attacks as that of Gentillet.

On the English stage the Machiavellian villain or 'the Machiavel' rapidly becomes a striking figure, one of the supreme embodiments of the idea of active evil in society. He thus joined forces with the archvillain of the medieval English liturgical drama, Satan himself.

The end-result, for tragedy, has been suggested
by Jan Kott (in *Shakespeare Our Contemporary*, 1964),
speaking of the vision projected in *King Lear*, the
bleakest of Shakespeare's great tragedies and probably
the one in which he comes nearest to seeing eye to eye
with such of his fellow-artists as Marlowe, Chapman,
Tourneur, or Webster. Active evil takes on heroic
scale and furious intensities. The broad theme of
"The decay and fall of the world" appears on two radically different stages. On the first (Mr. Kott terms
it "Macbeth's stage"), we see "only huge Renaissance
monsters, devouring one another like beasts of prey";
and in the more readily comprehensible part of many a
tragedy, "people murder, butcher and torture one
another, commit adultery and fornication, divide king-
doms" (Kott, pp. 153, 161). But all these sequences
of violence merely illustrate and exemplify what a
disintegrated social order has fallen to. The deeper
meaning of the major tragedies is worked out on another
symbolic stage (Kott terms it "Job's stage"), where the
protagonists, as well as the audience, may come to
realize the ultimate significance of the catastrophes
that have befallen them and, by empathy, us all.

Our sketch of the workings of the English tragic
sense of life before the heyday of the Elizabethan
tragic theatre is almost done. Two points still need
comment. Both concern stoicism as a philosophy of life,
and both represent the living force strong books can
exert. Little known now but popular with the Elizabethan intelligentsia, including Queen Elizabeth herself (she made a translation), was the *Consolations of
Philosophy* by Boethius (*ca.* A.D. 480-524). King
Alfred (A.D. 849-899) himself treasured it so much that
he translated it into Anglo-Saxon.

Let us rather be down to earth than technical.
The heart of the Stoic philosophy, to Englishmen from
Beowulf's and King Alfred's time to that of the Elizabethan tragic heroes, was to make a "virtue of necessity," to fight steadfastly against evil, to be self-
reliant and to achieve the highest possible human

dignity through disciplined use of one's fullest powers. "Keep a stiff upper lip"--"never say die"--
"The English, in war, lose every battle except the
last one" (which decides all!)--these stoical cliches
echo through English history. Treasured by the Middle Ages, the *Consolations of Philosophy* gained even
wider power when in print.

But the essentials of a Stoic philosophy of life,
so congenial to Englishmen, came to the Elizabethans
even more strongly through dramatic and other writings of Seneca (*ca*. 3 B.C.-A.D. 65). And Seneca had
more than a hang-tough philosophy for would-be tragic
playwrights. In all our sketch of the English tragic
spirit, we have so far seen no artist who really knew
how to structure a tragedy for the living stage. From
the rather static English tragedy, *Gorboduc* (1562) to
the 1581 publication of the collection, *Seneca His
Tenne Tragedies Translated*, there were many experi-
ments in structuring drama along tight, controlled
and Senecan lines.

First, Seneca could show that plot must have
shape, must focus on a central theme and exclude ir-
relevant matter, must have simplicity and clarity.
(This last countered the Elizabethan taste for over-
complexity.) He showed how directness and logical
plot-development could be provided, that great actions must be prepared for. He showed a view of tragedy as the strife of a human being against the forces
of his character or of 'fate.' He suggested concen-
tration on psychology and on emotional states of being
rather than upon external events. He suggested (but
few Elizabethans followed) simplicity of the final
action in the drama. He developed interest in talk,
in extended eloquence, and in ethical speeches which
may challenge writer, actor, and audience to rise to
heights of intense imaginative experience; although,
before reading Seneca, Elizabethans had already come
to enjoy complex spoken poetic language. If the long
speech in Elizabethan drama is not purely a result of

Senecan influence, it at last developed in harmony
with the extended lyric sequences found in Senecan
tragedy. Both Seneca's tragedies and his *Moral
Essays*, also widely known, enlarged the existing interest in the dramatic use of maxims and epigrams
which could offer pithy compressed opinions of life's
meaning.

But finally, it must be said that serious English tragedy, from Kyd's *Spanish Tragedy* onwards, is
largely a native growth. Such influences as Seneca's
can easily be exaggerated, as T. S. Eliot wisely re-
marked (*Elizabethan Essays*; introd. to Tudor Translations edition of the *Tenne Tragedies*). *The Spanish
Tragedy* presents bloody events on stage (hence the
term 'tragedy of blood'), which Seneca did not.
Seneca does not have plot in the sense that Kyd does.
Puzzled as to why so much Elizabethan tragedy was
"sanguinary" to the end of the drama (1640), whereas
the old morality plays (e.g., *Everyman*) were not,
Eliot fell back on the guess that this represented
"Italian" influence, to which Kyd and others added a
native talent for ingenuity of plot. Rather too casually, we think, Eliot surmised that the revenge tragedies of blood (*Spanish Tragedy, Hamlet*, etc.) grati-
fied Elizabethan low-brow audiences by a "release of
restraint," thus giving them a pleasure comparable to
that now offered the press and television public by
reports and views of violent crime.

To sum up, for centuries before the great tragic
drama began in Elizabethan England, Englishmen had,
in their own peculiar and increasingly nationalist
ways, developed a tragic sense of life. Built upon a
primitive base in Anglo-Saxon times, added to by the
'realism' and the romances of the Middle Age, this
sense of tragedy was greatly intensified by Renaissance and Reformation inquiries into human nature and
history. Perhaps only two things were lacking by
about 1585 to begin the development of really important and modern tragic drama. One was the appearance

of a widespread sense that the age had arrived at a
kind of profound moral crisis; and this sense can be
traced from at least the 1580s, while it became intense in the 1590s. The other requisite was the appearance of a seminal genius whose powers were suited
to the actual theatre and to the audience of the age.
Such a genius was Thomas Kyd, once known for a now-
lost play on Hamlet, now memorable for *The Spanish
Tragedy*.

VII   The Search for Justice

in an Often Corrupt Modern Power-State:

Thomas Kyd, *The Spanish Tragedy* (*ca.* 1585)

Kyd's Spanish Tragedy

It is not at all surprising that there was no
really popular interest in tragedy before Kyd's
Spanish Tragedy of about 1585. The Elizabethan intelligentsia unmistakably enjoyed didactic adapta-
tions of Seneca, from *Gorboduc* (performed 1562) onwards. If their tastes had prevailed, there would
never have been any significant and still-living, or

Criticism:

Fredson Bowers, *Elizabethan Revenge Tragedy*. 1940.

Juliet Dusinberre, *Shakespeare and the Nature of
Women*. (On the status of women in the English
Renaissance). Harper & Row, 1975.

Tucker Brooke and M. Shaaber, *The Renaissance*.
Meredith, 1967.

Philip Edwards, "The Spanish Tragedy," in *Shakespeare's Contemporaries*, ed. Bluestone. 1961
(paperback).

Willard Farnham, *The Medieval Heritage of Elizabethan Tragedy*.

Irving Ribner, *Jacobean Tragedy: The Quest for
Moral Order*.

Theodore Spencer, *Shakespeare and the Nature of Man*.

E. M. W. Tillyard, *The Elizabethan World-Picture*.

potentially living, work in tragic drama. We think
the same comment on restrictive tastes fits such high-
level intellectuals as the Sir Philip Sidney of the
Apology for Poetry (probably written *ca.* 1583), with
its mockery of what he took to be the English drama
for its failure to conform to the so-called unities
of time, place, and action which the neo-classic
critics had already begun to sanctify. Very oddly
and very fortunately, the major Elizabethans were not
over-awed by the prestige of the classics.

Critics who love tradition delight to point out
that Thomas Kyd learned much about conventional devices and tragic themes from Seneca or (broadly) the
Italians. But Kyd's own novel applications and inventions are far more notable than the mere facts of his
borrowings.

First, *The Spanish Tragedy* imaginatively projects
what to its audiences was a contemporary story, a hot
and lurid play of modern war, of passionate (and not
Petrarchan) love. In dramatic settings (or imagined
locales), manners, and morals, the action suggests
what to Elizabethans was credible for contemporary
Spain of the moment. Modern critics have learned that
Kyd's plot is his own invention. To its first audiences it was dramatically offered as a complex of
events which followed the historic battle of Alcantara,
in the early 1580s.

Second, where the earlier Senecan tragic models
held to a simple storyline, Kyd designed a complex
dramatic structure. The later Elizabethans strongly
liked involved stories—two or three lines of action
developed simultaneously. *The Spanish Tragedy* provides a busy "wilderness of subplots" and livens them
up with enough theatrically hair-raising "tricks and
turns to make the fortune" of a detective-story writer
of today (Brooke).

Thirdly, Kyd shows the first truly theatrically
inventive mind in English tragedy. The Elizabethan

92

popular-stage, beginning with its crude inn-yard form, emerges as one of the few great inventions of places-for-dramatic-playing in the world's theatrical history. On its lowest platform-level, it offered four sites for action (the outer-below; the inner-below; the two side-doors). Then on the floor above were an inner-above stage space and, at the sides, two window-stages (or bay windows) from which actors could look down on and speak to those below them--and of course to the audience. This Elizabethan public theatre, in short, provided the many potentialities of a multi-level stage. And such multi-level stages may be used to represent to the audience several planes or levels of conscious-ness, or several aspects of a story, at the same time. No one before Thomas Kyd seems to have realized these multiple possibilities.

But Kyd, in the *Spanish Tragedy*, evidently thought, felt, and wrote to offer the reader and audi-ence drama at all levels of this popular stage. (Bethel's *Shakespeare and the Popular Dramatic Tradi-tion* is acute on the multi-planes of consciousness and on ways by which audiences had learned to respond to them). In the older 'Senecan' plays (e.g., *Gorboduc*) little action occurs onstage; the most in-teresting events are imagined to happen offstage, after which a messenger reports them.

Not so with Kyd. In the course of *The Spanish Tragedy* he invents stage action and stage 'business' in almost fantastic quantities. And when offstage action does occur, Kyd lets us see the result onstage. Kyd is the first notable English *theatrical* poet. His imagination framed a drama as both an oral and a vis-ual spectacle of men and passions in conflict, well adapted to theatrical conditions. Thus his tragedy provided the audience with no less than nine murders and suicides, spaced with cunning and variety. Not to mention a public hanging (Pedringnano, sentenced by the hero, Hieronymo, in his role as justice); a burning at the stake whose horrid consummation is only

93

averted in the nick of time (III.i), with the flames
already crackling; an elderly gentlewoman, mother of
a murder victim, runs lunatic (IV.i); and a father,
triumphant at last in his pursuit of justice, bites
out his tongue (V.iii). With all these, he invented
(as Brooke said) endless other "devices to prevent
tediousness." The older Senecan plays had pantomimed
or 'dumb' shows, some of which Kyd keeps (as when the
figure of Revenge and the Ghost of Don Andrea watch
a marriage or Hymen-figures blow out two "nuptial
torches" and quench them with blood (IV.vii).

The play-within-the-play (V.iii), which effects
the final catastrophe, however, was Kyd's own theatrical invention. It is deftly managed to produce
strange emotions, all sensed by the audience. To the
noble spectators on stage, it is a fashionable court
entertainment, which they react to as to a work of
make-believe well-acted out. To some of the partici-
pants (Balthasar and the villain Lorenzo) it is also
a game, until they are stabbed indeed. To Hieronimo,
who has devised this means of public revenge in order
to secure his aim of justice, it is just that, only
at first masked as a show. To the heroine Bel-
Imperia, who understands Hieronimo's plan, the play
within the play achieves two cherished aims--revenge
and her own suicide, which Hieronimo had not planned.
The reader of Shakespeare's *Hamlet* may compare for
himself the uses to which the play-within-the-play
was put in the later tragedy of revenge.

As a brilliant theatrical poet, Kyd first recognized and richly used the hitherto unsurmised potentiality of the Elizabethan public stage for moving
the audience by controlled effects of multi-conscious-
ness. Fine instances come in II.iv. and in IV.iv.
The first of these scenes effects the on-stage murder
of Horatio and its discovery by his father and mother.
There is a novel three-ring effect. On the main stage
Horatio and Bel-Imperia discuss intimate affairs and
tentatively make love; meanwhile a brutally ironic

94

counterpoint is supplied by the reactions and comments of secret onlookers (Prince Balthasar, Lorenzo, Pedringnano) who overhear the lovemaking and provide a little death-music; and all the while, from 'above' (but quite visible to the audience) the supernatural figures of Revenge and the ghost of Don Andrea brood on the whole spectacle. Thus with fine and many-leveled irony, the audience can sense and enjoy the emotions of all three groups *simultaneously*.

Fourth, *The Spanish Tragedy* projects onstage not only emotionally charged and psychologically credible characters, but its action brings into conflict people whose twists of imagined personality are eccentric, strange, lurid, and sometimes fantastic. Brooke is quite right: "The Elizabethans liked queer people," or eccentrics, as the English still do to this day-- almost any good long walk through London testifies to this. High-level academic analyses of formal Elizabethan psychologies (L. Babb's *The Elizabethan Malady* [excessive melancholy], (1951) is best) tend to lead the reader away from this obvious fact. So, for comedy, do the frequent, tedious expositions of the 'four humours' psychology, as applicable to Jonsonian comedy. These too-rigid formalizations indicate an academic disease or excess. No good working playwright has as his business the exposition of theories of psychology (e.g., for today, post-Freudian?). Like the best Elizabethan tragic writers, Kyd seems to have been aware that his work was first to observe people in their variety, then to put a selection of them onstage for our pleasure.

To illustrate Kyd's dramatization of queer people:

--Even the Ghost of Don Andrea is individualized in his passionate response to Hell's horrors (I-Chorus);

--Balthazar's amorousness for the unwilling Bel-Imperia is oddly whetted by proximity to the scene and event of Horatio's murder (II.iv. 51-60);

95

--Lorenzo is a light-hearted, not a 'heavy'
villain. Embodying Machiavellian cunning and ruthlessness, he enjoys doing so. An accomplished villain, he has a talent for dissembling (a useful
theatrical device, as well as a political), and he
relishes the humor of the evil situations he brings
about;

--Old Hieronymo is obscurely mad, and in madness
(like Lear, later), he sees truth more clearly than
ever before (e.g., IV.vi);

--Villupo (I.ii and III.i) is the 'heavy' vil-
lain--i.e., excessively obvious;

--Bel-Imperia, the heroine of the piece (contrast the vapidity of Ophelia!) is, as Brooke wittily
said, "that ever new and dreaded portent, the 'new'
woman, who flouts the mores with a lethal charm." We
would observe that the thing she seeks, taking the
initiative in love-making, is union with the man she
personally respects and cherishes (Horatio); the
"mores" she seems to rebel against is the traditional
pattern of the political, arranged marriage. She
thus emerges as the first 'romantic' heroine of the
Elizabethan or modern theatre.

--Even the villainous Lorenzo's page-boy is an
odd character, queerly funny and equally callous as
he enjoys the jest by which Pedringnano gets hung.
Throughout the buildup to the hanging, the boy helps
out with lively satiric pantomime (pointing mock-
encouragingly to the box which Pedringnano mistakenly
believes holds his last-minute pardon), at once comic
and horrible;

--There are ironic twists and oddities of theatre.
For instance, the old Father who appeals to Judge
Hieronymo for justice (IV.vii.302-321) closely resembles, to Hieronymo's partly-mad eyes, his murdered
son Horatio. (I surmise the actor who played Horatio
re-appeared, 'doubling' roles, as the old Father.)

--Freakish twists in relationships appear. For
instance, the conventionally 'good' Duke of Castile
has, as his son, the viciously ambitious villain,
Lorenzo (e.g., IV.vii.40-95). (One might compare
the sequence in Shakespeare's *Lear* wherein the deceit-
ful son, Edmund, dupes his too-trusting father,
Gloucester.)

Fifth, I suggest that Kyd's *Spanish Tragedy* is
remarkable for its peculiarly Elizabethan and dramatic
achievement in poetic style. Try to imagine seeing
and hearing this play in the open air (as the Elizabethan public theatres were open to the sky), and
voiced, not by introspective, inward-looking small-
voiced modern lyric poets, but rather by strong popular actors equipped with 'big' voices and a fairly
wide range of emotional control. Open-air acoustics
as well as the then-popular audience (comparable to
New York's Central Park audiences today?) required
actors able to cope with a powerful oratorical style.

Such an actor was the Edward Alleyn who first
played Hieronymo, or the Burbage who first played
Hamlet. For such actors, Thomas Kyd explored and
crystallized what has been termed by Brooke, with
right admiration, a "ranting style." Not to dive
into controversies overmuch here, we identify such a
spoken poetic-theatrical style as firmly controlled
but boldly extroverted, like a Beethoven symphonic
crescendo.

As instances of Kyd's search for a 'big' style--
a search of course not always successful--we may cite
these instances:

--The somber, atmospheric choral opening;

--The General's narrative of the war just past
(I.iii.60+);

--Bel-Imperia's soliloquy (I.iii.60+), in which
she is swiftly drawn as a woman of complex, violent

emotions which blend sorrow for her dead fiance, violent desire for revenge on his killer Balthazar, and
new-found fascination with Horatio. Kyd's smoldering
verse catches her moods.

--Hieronymo's anguished speeches as he discovers
his son murdered (II.iv);

--Hieronymo's theatrically famous soliloquy
(III.ii), in which Kyd daringly continues the mood of
the discovery-scene (II.iv), as a musical motif might
re-enter in Beethoven;

--There is perhaps no need to illustrate further.
The reader may for himself find other instances of
Kyd's control of a bold theatrical style of expression.

Summing up, *The Spanish Tragedy* is distinctively
appealing artistically for (1) the careful building of
its main plot and sub-plot; (2) its subtle and ironic
action; (3) the Machiavellian villain, Lorenzo; (4)
the suffering heroine, Bel-Imperia; (5) the revenge
themes, with revenge becoming equal to justice; (6) the
hesitating avenger (Hieronymo), who has to search out
the wrong-doers and ascertain their identity before
proceeding; (7) the use of staged madness, both real
(Hieronymo's shortly after discovering his son's murder
and partly during his court-sitting as justice); and
pretended (e.g., IV.iv, when Hieronymo is mistaken
for a 'real' madman); (8) the onstage dramatization
of multiple murders and other physical horrors; (9) the
use of pantomimed 'dumb shows' as well as the Kydian
invention of the play-within-the-play; (10) its powerful and, in the best sense, "ranting" style of theatrical speech.

Lastly (11) there is the peculiar Kydian tragic
irony to be considered. Bowers thinks (*Elizabethan
Revenge Tragedy*), I believe rightly, that Elizabethan
tragedy at last became "entirely a native drama," to
which English audiences could give full-range responses
and sympathies, when, in the middle of *The Spanish
Tragedy*, we are asked to sympathize with the search

for justice for one (Horatio) murdered before our
eyes, not reminiscently in the remote past, as with
Senecan drama.

This sense of tragic immediacy and modern relevance is, paradoxically, intensified by Kyd's sense
of irony, his special tragic perspective. Philip
Edwards (Introduction to the 'Revels Plays' ed.)
reasons that an alert audience, after hearing the
Act I-Chorus (pp. 5-6 in *Tragedy*) would see that the
play's decisive action began, not with the onstage
murder of Horatio (in II.iv), but rather with the
dishonorable killing of Don Andrea by Balthazar in
the war concluded just before the play's action begins, as we learn from the victim-as-ghost.

Thereafter, Edwards reasons, the whole play may
be seen as "built upon irony, upon the ignorance of
the characters that they are being used to fulfill the
decree of the gods." For, from the Act I-Chorus, the
audience knows this decree, but no personage within
the main play does. Thus the characters, ironically,
always have mistaken notions about the end toward
which their actions are leading them. Bel-Imperia
believes that "second love will further her revenge;"
and so it does, but only, as it turns out, through
the murder of her second love, Horatio. Thus, as
Horatio and Bel-Imperia speak of consummating their
mutual passion (II.ii), they are overheard by those
plotting to destroy them. And as the happy and un-
witting lovers go offstage (II.iii), the King enters,
complacently planning the politically expedient marriage of Bel-Imperia with Prince Balthazar. Thus the
Machiavellian villain Lorenzo betrays to Hieronymo
his murder of Horatio by the very means he chooses to
keep it secret—by the destruction of his accomplices.
Thus the accomplice and minor villain, Pedringnano,
is secure in his trust of his master, Lorenzo, who is
about to have him killed. And thus the entire court
and the King, in the play's grand wind-up scene (V.iii)
"applaud the acting in a play (within-the-play) in
which the deaths are real."

VIII   Scientific Genius and the Lust for

            Total Power and Knowledge:

   Christopher Marlowe, *Doctor Faustus* (? 1591-93)

     Within an incredibly brief time, a mere six years
(1586-1593), Marlowe changed the whole main course of
modern tragedy.   Shakespeare may have given Marlowe
some ideas for *Edward II* (see P. Alexander, *Times*
(London) *Literary Supplement*, April 2, 1964), but
otherwise Marlowe was the bold pioneer.   Some of his
greatest artistic achievements may be summed up here.

Suggested Listening and Criticism

     The 'Caedmon' recording, with Frank Silvera in
     the title role.

     John Bakeless. *Christopher Marlowe*. Morrow,
     1937.

     Roy Battenhouse. *Tamburlaine*. Vanderbilt UP,
     1964.

     Frederick Boas. *Christopher Marlowe*. Clarendon,
     1940.

     Douglas Cole. *Suffering and Evil in the Plays of
     Christopher Marlowe*. Princeton, 1962.

     Una Ellis-Fermor. *Christopher Marlowe*. Methuen,
     1927.

     J. Leslie Hotson. *The Death of Christopher
     Marlowe*. London, 1925.

     Leo Kirschbaum. "Marlowe's Faustus: A Reconsid-
     eration," *Review of English Studies*, XIX (1943),
     225-241.

First is what Ben Jonson justly termed Marlowe's
"mighty line." "Infinite riches in a little room!"
(*Jew of Malta*) exemplifies it. For most of the 16th
century, poets had experimented with poetic lines of
almost every conceivable metrical pattern and length,
even including the now-absurd "fourteener" (one line
of 14 syllables). Marlowe resolved the controversy
once and for all by his dazzling demonstration that
the unrhymed iambic pentameter, the "blank verse"
line, had greater potentialities for dramatic use
than any other competing form. In *The Spanish Tragedy*, Thomas Kyd, at about the same time as Marlowe,

Paul Kocher. *Christopher Marlowe*. University
of N. Carolina, 1946.

*Harry Levin. *The Overreacher: A Study of
Christopher Marlowe*. Harvard, 1952. (If you
want to reach just one, make this it). Paperback.

M. M. Mahood. "Marlowe's Heroes," *Poetry and
Humanism*. London, 1950, pp. 54-86. (Sensitive;
Catholic viewpoint.)

Marlowe: A Collection of Critical Essays, ed.
Clifford Leech. Prentice-Hall, 1964. Paperback.

James Smith. "Marlowe's Dr. Faustus," *Scrutiny*,
VIII (1939), 36-55.

Eugene Waith. *The Herculean Hero in Marlowe,
Chapman, Shakespeare and Dryden*. Columbia, 1962.

had used the blank verse line strongly, but without the flexibility, range, and poetic power of Marlowe. (See, for instance, in *Spanish Tragedy*, III.ii.1-24, with Hieronimo's soliloquy beginning "O eyes! no eyes, but fountains fraught with tears" etc.)

Every major dramatic artist of the Renaissance, after Marlowe, made the blank verse line his chief instrument of expression.. And poets down to our own day (Milton, Wordsworth, etc.) have been unable to find a better verse for supreme eloquence in English. The opening and closing scenes of *Doctor Faustus* may serve as most memorable instances of Marlowe's verse-mastery.

Secondly, Marlowe is credited with the virtual creation of the 'Romantic' drama and especially of tragedy. In *The Spanish Tragedy*, compelling as may be Hieronimo's anguished search for justice on earth, this search is kept within the bounds of a recent Renaissance court. Moreover, while at first Hieronimo is balked, because all normal channels of justice are closed to him, in the end, although having to take justice into his own hands, he succeeds publicly in bringing the malefactors to their deserved retribution. At times the Marshal of Spain, the bereaved father, cries out against the seeming indifference of "the Heavens" to his struggle. But in the end a somewhat terrible justice is done. Hence one might view the spectacle spread before us by Kyd as a grimly encouraging one, warranting the humanist optimism anchored to the idea that the modern age exists under watchful divine eyes and powers which, in the end, befriend those who search and struggle for justice on earth.

Marlowe, our first grand-scale romantic dramatist, shows however virtually no interest in such localized concerns and questions, which might seem relatively smug and small, however urgent to those involved. He ignored the currently-fashionable themes of his day, ignored the artfully-worked out tiny world of the lover's pains, celebrated by many Elizabethan lyricists; ignored the world of polite society, which a John Lyly spread before sophisticates in his dainty prose in a pseudo-novel, *Euphues* etc. A Robert Greene found a ready public for his gritty exposés of every-day commonplace crime and low-life, or evil living, all of which Marlowe ignored.

We agree with Tucker Brooke that Marlowe's plays show him to have had a caustic, penetrating bent of mind. Turning away from relatively petty issues of the age, he rather strove to deal with ever-expanding visions of life which broke all hitherto-known bounds and limits. Thus his central themes are, first, the *Tamburlaine* theme, that of lust for regal, then universal and total dominion and power. Also in *Tamburlaine* we meet the strangely heroic theme of friendship outlasting even death (e.g., I *Tamburlaine*, II.1.242+). Love-themes, in *Tamburlaine* and in *Doctor Faustus*, as in the old Tristan-Isolde romance, show love almost as a consuming fire, poetically transcending death itself. *Doctor Faustus*, even in the imperfect text which survives, takes as its theme lust-for-knowledge, exceeding all bounds, profane and sacred alike. And in all Marlowe's major tragedies appears the central figure of the 'Faustian' hero, the man of genius who insatiably is driven to reject the very idea of limits, of rest. This has been aptly termed the "over-reacher" theme and hero. In *Tamburlaine* the hero gives it wondrous expression, as he pursues a controlling vision of the mystery which lies unknown before him, the mystery and fascination of

. . . . Life which
Will us to wear ourselves and never rest.

(*I Tamb.* 1.877)

The Marlovian tragic drama thus follows actions which evolve from some mighty ruling passion or profound drive. There is virtually no interest whatever

103

in neat evolution of plot (Shakespeare commits himself to plots as a rule). The central concern is
rather with passions and ideas in juxtaposition and
conflict. Insofar as something recognizable as plot
survives, its purpose tends to be to produce situations of wide range and varied intensities, in which
the dramatic characters can say and do what would
otherwise be either impossible for them or unintel-
ligible to the audience. Marlowe searches for themes
and characters which are 'great' and 'heroic' on all
levels. The ruling conception of human greatness and
heroism, however, in Marlowe radically departs from
the major English Renaissance Christian humanist tradition.

Embodied in his tragedies of the "over-reacher"
is the concept of the essential Marlovian hero. At a
time when many poets still were admiringly attracted
by the vanishing world of medieval chivalry and chivalric romance (Shakespeare, Spenser), Marlowe offered
more modern imaginations an almost staggeringly un- or
anti-chivalric image of credible human greatness.
Looking about him at late Renaissance civilization,
Marlowe's tragic vision centered, not on the (to him)
obsolete drama of honor, but rather on the naked
struggle for power on a world-wide scale.

His figure of Tamburlaine seems frankly to glor-
ify the man whose genius is best expressed, at whatever cost to long-suffering humanity, in unlimited
imperial struggles for domination of mankind. The
very quintessence of Tamburlaine's sinister genius is
exactly the idea, ascribed to Machiavelli, that might
makes right. So Tamburlaine strides across the world-
stage, great in audacity, in ruthlessness, in amoral
political cunning, in the magnificence of his vision
of boundless ambition. For such a figure, almost by
definition there can be no point of rest while new
worlds remain to be conquered. True, the audience is
at liberty to moralize such a spectacle and to de-
nounce the supreme conqueror, as indeed his victims do,
small comfort though it is to them.

With this daring modern drama of power and ambition comes a strange alteration of tragic humor
and eroticism. Vanished is the comparatively simple,
almost undergraduate humor of Shakespeare's Prince
Hal romping with Falstaff in Eastcheap dives. We do
not agree with critics who would deny to Marlowe a
sense of comedy. But what appears is conqueror-humor,
frequently hard, often cruel, sometimes witty, rarely
if ever compassionate (e.g., as in the revel-scenes
in *I Tamburlaine* IV; or in the rough practical jokes
played at the Papal court in *Faustus*). Eroticism also
becomes epic: e.g., in the grandeur and terror of
Tamburlaine's evocation of Zenocrate's beauty, set
against the ruthless destruction of Damascus as a
backdrop; or in *Faustus*, the hero's dazzling apostrophe
to beauty, when the dream-vision of Helen of Troy is
silently passed before our eyes:

Was this the face that launch'd a thousand ships,
And burnt the topless towers of Ilium?...
O, thou art fairer than the evening air
Clad in the beauty of a thousand stars;...(V.i.94+)

Thirdly, to Marlowe is due the credit for the
"discovery of the secret of dramatic action" (Brooke),
that is of a poetic and theatrical means by which a
grand-scale modernly romantic drama can be projected
on actual stages. The distinctive discovery is that
the poetry itself, the words, must be used as the
symbols of the action. For any stage which limits
representation of human experience to that which can
be shown physically is bound, in the end, by a narrow,
cramping form of so-called realism. From *Tamburlaine*
to *The Jew of Malta* to *Doctor Faustus*, Marlowe may be
seen working out a highly controlled, intricate, sup-
ple and strongly expressive kind of stagecraft, anchored to the poetry, growing in precision and subtle-
ty.

Moreover, Marlowe is rightly seen as the "decisive genius" who first explored the world of modern
tragic values in English drama. First in Marlowe is

found dramatized "the significant schism between the ideal or spiritual world and the world pragmatically estimated by everyday observation"--a schism "which seems, in one form or another, to be an essential part of any tragic conception of the universe." First sensed in *Tamburlaine*, this crucial insight is fully operative in *Doctor Faustus*, where the "possibility of reconciling the course of man's life with the aspiration of his spiritual instincts is rejected." So, in the grimly beautiful last act, Faustus perceives an ultimate and appalling irony:

> ...Belike we must sin and so consequently die.
> Aye, we must die an everlasting death...die eternally.

Thus, as Marlowe's tragic vision has it, "The separation between the two worlds [of the spirit and of materialism] is complete....The total of man's experience is thereafter no true [unified] universe but a battleground, a dual presentation of mutually contradictory experiences." (Ellis-Fermor, *Jacobean Drama*, 1936, pp. 5-17).

In thus defining the fundamental mood and direction of English tragedy, Marlowe exerted indirectly a strong effect also upon the delimitation of the field and mood of comedy. This will eventually appear, around 1600, in the new directions in drama of which Ben Jonson is the master spirit, with his comedy of the over-reacher.

On Marlowe's *Doctor Faustus*

Marlowe's strange tragedy survives in two often-differing texts, but the controversy over them need not concern us here. The version in the *Tragedy* Text is essentially the 1604 quarto. At least three kinds of material can fairly readily be seen: (1) farce or clownage; (2) comic or marvelous incident; (3) tragic action, which often is intermixed especially with the marvelous. Among critics there has long been hot argument on how much of each kind of drama Marlowe probably wrote (there is always the possibility that actors added stuff of their own; English clowns were especially notorious for this—see Hamlet's sharp warning to the players to avoid such outrages, in *Hamlet*, III.ii.40-47). And controversy is equally hot over what Marlowe meant when he wrote *Dr. Faustus*, for his dramatic methods are as individualized as his tragic vision.

"Farce or clownage" would include these bits:

--Wagner and the clown (I.iv);

--The clowns with Faustus' book (II.iii);

--The clowns with the Vintner and the burlesque invocation (III.ii);

--The horse-trader's ("courser's") bargain and the horse-trader cheated (IV.ii).

Comic or marvelous incident includes:

--The Chorus by Wagner (begins act III);

--The arrival of Faustus and Mephistophilis in Rome (III.i);

--Faustus is made invisible (III.i.60 to end);

--The interrupted Papal banquet and the solemn cursing (III.i);

--The Chorus which begins Act IV;

--The apparition of the Emperor Alexander (IV.i.80+); with this the jeering knight who is magically 'horned';

--Wagner brings news (IV.ii.100+);

--Wonders of Vanholt, with the magic grapes (IV.iii);

--Farewell to Vanholt (end IV.iii).

Finally there is the tragic action which is the heart of the play; it principally comprises (this is what is mainly heard in Frank Silvera's "Caedmon" recording):

--Prologue and Chorus to Act I;

--Act I, as Faustus reviews his studies and decides to go all out for black magic. Wagner's mission. The Good and Bad Angels (who seem to speak to Faustus' subconsciousness). Faustus dreams of power. The petty magicians, Valdes and Cornelius, visit him. Wagner and the Scholars (I.ii). And the sinister climax--Faustus' evocation of Mephistophilis, with their disputation (I.iii).

--Act II. Faustus faces damnation. The Good and Bad Angels reappear. The infernal bond is signed in Faustus' blood. The devil-wife appears. The magic book. Continuous with these episodes

--Faustus and Mephistophilis dispute. The Good and Bad Angels come and go. Disputation continues. Lucifer intervenes. The Seven Deadly Sin appear. Another magic book is given to Faustus.

(Thus, except for the incident of Wagner and the clown, I.iv. the tragic action which dominates the first two acts (as far as II.ii) forms a powerful, fairly unified sequence. But then the center of the play, from II.iii through IV, is filled either with comic or miraculous incidents, or with "farce or clownage.")

--Act V resumes the power of Act I. It is almost wholly tragic material and includes some of Marlowe's most remarkable writing:

Wagner's foreboding (V.i). The students and the apparition of Helen of Troy. The Old Man's

fruitless exhortation. Mephistophilis re-
gains control and Faustus renews the bond.
Evocation of Helen (V.i). The Old Man is
assailed by devils. With V.ii, Faustus takes
leave of his students. Then comes Faustus'
last hour. And the tragic action ends with
the warning by the Choral Epilogue, to learn
from Faustus' "hellish fall" that the "wise"
will only "wonder at unlawful things

  Whose deepness doth entice such forward wits
  To practice more than heavenly power permits.

In other words, the point is finally made that
man's only chance for happiness depends upon his acceptance of the limits of humanity, and to try to
transcend them is a virtual guarantee of total disaster.

As used to happen to disputed parts of Shakespeare's texts (Coleridge's arbitrary effort to repu-
diate the drunken Porter's speech in *Macbeth* is a
notorious example, now itself repudiated), scholars
have puzzled over the very real text problem for *Dr.
Faustus*, trying their best to get at what Marlowe intended to write, as nearly as this is possible. Most
agree that neither the 1604 or the 1616 quarto is
wholly Marlowe's, for the likelihood of playhouse
tinkering with the text is strong.

I take a relatively conservative view, in agree-
ment with Kirschbaum: "'...there has been altogether
too much cocksureness in the determination of what is
Marlowe's and what is not....I am just as convinced
that he could and did write slapstick comic scenes
and uninspired serious scenes as I am that Shakespeare
could and did'" (L. Kirschbaum, cited by W. W. Greg,
Marlowe's 'Doctor Faustus' [1950], pp. 97-139 *passim.;*
see also pp. 16-17, whose 'elements' analysis we have
adapted.)

In a word, I suggest you assume that the *Doctor Faustus* printed in the *Tragedy* text represents substantially Marlowe's work and that you need not concern yourself with the alleged or real authorship problems.

Main Structural Movements of *Dr. Faustus*

Accordingly the play as it stands before you falls into three large structural movements. The first of these (Act I through II.ii; *Tragedy*, p. 62) traces part of one day and night in Faustus' life. Beginning with his arrogant rejection of all traditional studies, profane or sacred, it leads to his fierce choice of black magic (I.i; Note: a great many men, as late as the 1590s in England, still believed that what we call natural science was really a 'black', infernal, and anti-human art, the province of Satan & Co.). This leads to the sinister evocation of Mephistophilis (I.iii), so the fateful midnight appointment is made.

At this event, a grand intense stage-spectacle, we see the beauty and horror of Faustus' decision to sign an infernal bond, in his own blood. This done, we see him take his first tastes of the intoxicating powers and dreadful fears inherent in his new position in the universe, as a man wilfully cut off from God and totally committed to Lucifer. Faustus now first experiences agony of the spirit. We sense and see his self-horrified doubts and struggles with himself to "be resolv'd and ne'er repent" (II.ii), and his wildly cheerful acceptance of his committed status after the brief, savage visit from the terrible chief executive of Hell, Lucifer himself, first appalls, then entertains Faustus (now a duly initiated member of the club) with a cynically comic "Seven Deadly Sins" vaudeville act which puts Faustus in vast good humor.

Great Lucifer, then laying aside this temporary role as impresario, as a parting present gives Faustus

another book of magic and, with it, the sinister
polite assurance, "I will send for thee at midnight"
(i.e., when the 24-year bond is eventually forfeit).
Faustus is so dizzily joyful with his power and position that he hardly hears this parting shot. But he
does happily bid farewell to his mighty guests. (On
the Elizabethan stage, Lucifer and Belzebub probably
returned down the main trap door, while the inner-
below stage curtains were closed on Faustus' study,
with its books and scientific instruments.) So
Faustus, hugely pleased, exits with Mephistophilis
to begin his adventurous twenty-four years of imagined
limitless power through science, made available via
his pact with the devil.

The play's second main structural movement (from
II.iii through to the end of Act IV, in *Tragedy*)
traces episodically all but the last hours of the four-
and-twenty years of insights and powers for which
Faustus deeded away his immortal soul. Much of this
is comic and miraculous or magical incident, along with
many farcical and low-clownish bits. Frequently the
low-comic incidents indeed seem to burlesque or parody
the serious, tragic action in which Faustus appears
personally, usually with Mephistophilis. This parody
pattern indeed appears by I.iv (pp. 56-57), where
Wagner, a clownish oaf, hires a lousy ragged servant
and jeers that the "poor slave" would gladly "give his
soul to the Devil for a shoulder of mutton, though it
were blood-raw." To which the wretch tries absurdly
to achieve a touch of human dignity by declaring that
he would at least insist that the mutton be "well
roasted and good sauce to it"!

Many times, during this second major movement of
the play, Faustus seems content on stage simply to
amuse himself with contemplating the human comedy.
Very obviously (we shall return to this) the great man
is shown frittering away his time, doing none of the
grand actions, *either* humanly constructive *or* de-

structive, that he earlier found so deliriously happy
to anticipate, when he envisioned

> O what a world of profit and delight,
> Of power, of honor, of omnipotence
> Is promis'd to the studious artisan!
>   [i.e., to the supreme scientist]
> All things that move between the quiet poles
> Shall be at my command. Emperors and kings
> Are but obey'd in their several provinces,
> Nor can they raise the wind or rend the clouds;
> But his dominion that exceeds [excels] in this
> Stretcheth as far as doth the mind of man.
> A sound magician is a mighty god. (I.i.52-61)

Note also I.i.76-96 (p. 53). Or the sinister
glory of Faustus' dream of power "Be it to make the
moon drop from her sphere / Or the ocean to overwhelm
the world" (I.iii.41-42). Or his heroic ideas at
I.iii.96-116 (p. 56), etc. In contrast to Faustus'
early epic and tremendous ideas, the sleazy scientists
Valdes and Cornelius (I.i.119-146; pp. 53-54) are
petty men who only dream of vulgar get-rich-quick
schemes; they respect Faustus as a true intellectual
genius and hope he will cut them in on a share of the
world's loot.

The third and final structural movement of *Dr.
Faustus* is the short, grimly beautiful fifth Act,
which represents Faustus' final hours on earth. (It
also brings to our attention for the last time one
of the major questions which Faustus' career suggests:
namely, why does he not *repent*?) We hear of one last
desperate carouse, which shocks even the brutalized
Wagner. The silent vision of the fabulous Helen of
Troy is evoked by Faustus to please some former students of his. An 'Old Man,' a figure almost reeking
of mortality, appears and compassionately urges the
brooding scientific genius even now, late as it is,
to appeal to Christ for his mercy (V.i.37+), but
Faustus no longer has the nerve. With cynical humor,

Mephistophilis silently proffers Faustus a dagger,
in case he thinks suicide might help him. And
Faustus does make feeble gestures toward repentance,
only to collapse into ignominious cringing fear
before the concentrated fury of Mephistophilis
(V.i.69-71).

Finally (V.ii; pp. 71-73), Faustus is left on
stage, utterly alone, utterly despairing. And as the
great clock slowly marks the irrestible flow of time,
we see the last agonies of Faustus' spiritual bank-
ruptcy, his final recognition that for him there can
be no escape, and the deliberate horror of his last
moment before us. As the main-trap door (representing the regions of Hell; the Elizabethan theatre could
also manage stage-effects of smoke, flame etc.) slowly
opens--we hear Faustus' scream of imploration ("Ugly
hell, gape not!" 1.134). He begs wildly, "Come not,
Lucifer!" before the figures from below slowly appear;
he tries frantically to burn his books (they will not
burn), and collapses before the ultimate recognition
of his fate, in the awed whisper of "Ah! Mephistophilis!"

The Problem of a Comic Synthesis
as Related to Marlowe's Tragic Vision

How do the low-comic, burlesque, and related miraculous parts of this tragedy concern the lofty, passionate, and profoundly serious characterization of
the hero? Some critics (Kocher, for one) have attempted rather arbitrarily to dismiss the problem by
asserting that Marlowe *had* no sense of humor, hence
the linked assertion that the comedy was not written
by Marlowe at all but rather thrust in by unknown
writers seeking cheap laughter. I have already suggested as preferable the view that the entire text is
substantially Marlowe's.

Another too-obvious way of regarding comedy when
it appears in a tragedy is to think of it, as many do,
as so-called "comic relief." That is, the argument

goes, the audience may need a slight rest, a breather, and the clown's appearance (the drunken gate porter at Macbeth's castle, after Duncan's murder?) takes our minds off the hero's troubles briefly so that, when the action returns to them and the clown leaves the stage, we can pay even closer attention than might otherwise have been emotionally feasible. It is moreover a fact of dramatic history that Elizabethan playwrights, disregarding the outraged cries of neoclassicists such as Sir Philip Sidney, did frequently mix comedy and tragedy. By no means, however, always with success; and some of these clowneries are, to modern audiences, simply tedious if not downright stupefying--cheap horseplay dragged in by the heels.

I suggest that a comic synthesis, for *Dr. Faustus,* may strongly illuminate Marlowe's distinctive modern tragic vision. (Unless otherwise noted, quotes on this refer to R. Ornstein, in *ELH,* 22 [1955], 165-172.) First, the whole play has various comic levels, and "the slapstick scenes which tickled groundling fancies unite with the seemingly fragmented main action to form a subtly ironic tragic design" (165). But the usual Elizabethan practice was to let the clownery, the burlesque or parody (the "antimasque") *precede* the serious or tragic. Thus oafish servants might appear, aping and mocking the "manners and pretensions of their betters" (166), which stage device would help us to enjoy and understand the serious action when it came. The other-way round (serious first, burlesque or parody after it) would seem to be obviously deflating and anti-climactic. And clownery, then serious action, was indeed the usual Elizabethan stage pattern. Marlowe, in *Dr. Faustus,* however, seems to do the exact opposite.

At first sight it almost seems that, instead of enhancing the main action of his tragedy, he has reduced it "to absurdity scene by scene." How can he possibly hope to "magnify Faustus' achievements by having clowns parody them immediately afterwards"?

(167). Thus in a major episode we watch Faustus sell
his soul for knowledge, voluptuousness, and power,
whereupon, directly afterward, the Clown "considers
bartering his soul for a shoulder of mutton [just so
it's well-roasted!] and a taste of wenching." (167)
You can easily find many such examples of what at
first sight seems clearly a 'wrong' pattern.

Ornstein suggests that in *Faustus* Marlowe made
"an imperfect but brilliant invention" (166)--one
hardly apparent at first reading. Of course ironic
deflating humor can be reassuring to an audience for
at least two reasons: (1) that there may be "something infinitely reassuring in the clown who apes the
manner and the mannerisms of the superman" (167);
(2) that originally, when many still regarded science
as allied to diabolical magic, the clownish burlesques
and parodies would give audiences a kind of reassur-
ance through crude laughter, lest mortal fear overwhelm all esthetic and tragic response. But Ornstein
wittily suggests that the ironic comedy in *Dr. Faustus*
is much more than simply reassuring. "Its intention
...is both didactic and comic. Simultaneously non-
sensical and profound, it clarifies our perception of
moral values."

All of us normally, without thinking about it,
view the world through "the lenses of custom." Hence
"when false values pass current, even elemental truths
appear distorted, naive, or absurd." At first the
tragic ironist who deals with "elemental absurdities"
--such as eating children to cure poverty (Swift's
Modest Proposal) or, risking one's immortal soul for
a piece of well-roasted mutton--invites a tolerant
smile from those who assume that they have a "more
sensible and realistic appraisal of the world."

Comfortably, we smile, certain that modern, civilized society "does not and would not eat children."
(Did we then smile comfortably in 1968 when we heard
a commander in Vietnam, quite without irony, explain

115

that he had to destroy a village totally in order to save it?) In imagination or the theatre, viewing the action in *Dr. Faustus*, we are comfortably amused at the clown and the mutton, feeling certain that indeed "no man, however foolish, would damn his soul to satisfy his belly." (167-68)

O--we say to ourselves--he might damn his soul, as Faustus does, "to gain infinite power, yes, but we consider such ambition heroic"! (168) So thinks Ornstein, "We smile...only until we discover beneath the surface of our sensible view of life the grim absurdity depicted by the ironist--only until sensible or grandiose appearance and absurd reality melt into one." The tragic ironist is in effect "licensed to reveal 'absurd' truths only when he amuses his audience....Therefore Marlowe entertains us with Clowns and with the ancient but eternally successful comedy of futility." (168) (Is Lear's Fool often wiser than the King?) Probably what is called for is recognition that Marlowe, like Dickens in a sense, was a terribly honest comic and moral realist. We could make a similar point about Beckett of *Waiting for Godot* today. When this recognition is made, perhaps we can honestly face Marlowe's clowns as powerful "caricatures of the tragic hero" (168n).

We see the Clown feed his egotism with the idea of selling his soul for a chunk of mutton or a wench or so. Not accidentally, in the "crucial scene when Faustus first repents, Lucifer appears, impresario-like, with the Seven Deadly Sins"--a comic spectacle which Faustus "feeds" on, as he mocks these "harmless bogies of the superstitious mind." He is so "entranced by Lucifer's vaudeville show" that he "forgets salvation." Lucifer is also entertained but on a more intellectual plane. The consummate cynic, he diverts his victim with a picture-gallery that suggests Faustus' own futility." (168)

Of course the show of the Seven Deadly Sins was supposed to be amusing, as it was in much medieval literature. And we noted earlier that in the medieval English liturgical dramas, Satan appears as a comic villain, comic because the Catholic audience was assured that in the end the triumph of God's love was an absolute certainty. "In short the medieval mind knew the ludicrousness of insatiable desire. It knew that vice (to use Santayana's definition) is 'human nature strangled by the suicide of attempting the impossible.'" (168)

But by Marlowe's time in England, the firm assurances of the Middle Ages had become deeply and dangerously undermined. Knowing as much, perhaps, only Shakespeare of the greatest dramatists held fairly reassuringly to the older view of a divinely ordered universe (see E. Tillyard, *The Elizabethan World-Picture*).

But Marlowe's tragic vision, expressed in the characterization of Dr. Faustus, is far more radical and modern than most of Shakespeare's is. No "fustian villain ranting of his powers" (as the comic medieval Satan might do), Faustus is rather the image of a supremely intelligent man who, through the self-deceiving, progressive casuistry of his own wit and sensuality, ends by over-reaching himself. At the start of the play, Faustus speaks of plans which "though egocentric and grandiose, are constructive. He wants pleasure, riches, and power, but he also intends to make all learning his province, better the lot of students, improve geography, and defeat tyranny." (169) But these dreams of positive creativity remain only dreams. The "measure of his tragic fall is the increased disparity between his aspirations and his achievements." (170)

In the early part of the play, the Clown parodied Faustus' ideas and ambitions. But in the latter half, by a splendid Marlovian tragic irony, Faustus parodies them himself on stage. Thus eventually "we discover beneath the exalted appearance of the fearless rebel

the figure of the fool....The difference between hero
and clown is one of degree, not of kind." (170) It
is no more absurd to sell one's soul for supposedly
infinite power than for belly cheer. If anything, in
this comparison, Faustus' ambition is the more ridiculous because the less "realistic."

Thus the grand tragic irony which emerges from
this comic synthesis is that of a hero who tries to
become a god and in so doing becomes "less than a man."
Moreover, Ornstein observes, Marlowe shows us a Faustus
who makes on earth a personal nihilistic and almost
Dostoevskian hell of negation before the devils appear
to remove him in the end. (Modern man, his own worst
enemy in the major thrust of non-Shakespearean tragic
vision, no longer needs the gods and devils of the
past: he is quite capable of making his own hells on
earth while he lives.)

Thus the play's supreme irony appears in the last
scene when, madly, "Faustus would escape the negation
of hell by annihilating body and soul. The diseased
creative will succumbs at last to frenzied desire for
self-destruction." (172) But in the end, Faustus is
not God's fool but his own and Lucifer's. "*Doctor
Faustus*, then, is not the tragical history of a
glorious rebellion. For Marlowe shared with his ad-
miring contemporary, George Chapman, the disenchanted
vision of the aspiring mind--the knowledge that the
Comic Spirit hovers over the Icarian flight of the
self-announced superman." (172)

IX Affections' Storm--the New Tragedy of Passion

versus Reason in the Modern Power-State:

George Chapman's Original *Bussy d'Ambois*

(1600-1604)[*]

After Christopher Marlowe, George Chapman, in
his one masterpiece, is the most forward-looking or
'modern' of Renaissance playwrights. Long antici-
pating Freud, Chapman pioneered the kind of tragedy
in which what may be called moral man is pitted
against immoral or amoral society. In many respects,
a very stimulating comparison may be made between
Bussy D'Ambois and Hamlet as tragic heroes, between
Tamyra and Ophelia as heroines.

----

[*]The play exists in two quite different forms--
the first, tragic, the second at best melodramatic.
The *Tragedy* anthology, unfortunately, prints the
second form, muddled together with the first. Strongly recommended therefore is either of these editions
of the original play: that by Maurice Evans in the
"New Mermaid" series (1966), or, best of all, that by
Nicholas Brooke in the "Revels Plays" series (1964;
Methuen). Criticism is confused because many equate
two different plays as the same. But see Brooke in
his edition; also Robert P. Adams, "Critical Myths
and Chapman's Original *Bussy D'Ambois,*" *Renaissance
Drama IX*, ed. S. Schoenbaum (Northwestern University
Press, 1967), pp. 141-161.

By and large, Chapman is remarkable for his psychological realism, for his concept of a tragic hero, and even more, perhaps, for his concept of a tragic heroine; for his figure of Tamyra had previously been paralleled only by the bold femme fatale of Kyd's *Spanish Tragedy* of *ca*. 1585, Bel-Imperia. Chapman is further memorable for the powerful and flexible control he was able to exert over styles (varied to express character and situation), over the complete dramatic structure or tragic design, and over characterization itself. Again, long before Freud, Chapman is notable for the clarity and depth of his insights into the pervasive power of sexuality in modern society.

There is no point here in going into the marked differences between the two existing versions of *Bussy D'Ambois* (the 1607, the 1641 posthumous text). Let it suffice that the major final effect of the changes is to leave the original play as tragedy, to turn the posthumous play toward "melodrama (rigged out with tragic trappings)..." (Brooke)

The original play is superior poetically, theatrically, in terms of character development, in its psychological realism, and in the clarity with which it transmits a tragic vision still meaningful today.

The dramatic and thematic structure of *Bussy D'Ambois* [hereafter meaning the 1607 text, or *'Bussy I'*] is remarkably clear and strong. The hero, a well-known man of resolute character and action, returns from self-imposed retirement (I.i) to a court (I.ii) where corruption is rife beneath a surface veneer of seeming honor and decency. The King's brother, Monsieur, who brought Bussy to court, has the covert objective of securing supreme power for himself, by inference through cutting the "thread" (i.e., the King's life) which separates Monsieur from power, should more devious means fail.

120

A serial critique of the play shows a large part
of Acts I-III, in the public sector of the action, to
be dominated by a subtle struggle on the part of the
just and strong King Henry, against the would-be
tyrant Monsieur. Indeed by III.ii, the King has won
Bussy over to his side as his aide or "Eagle," licensed publicly to expose corruption wherever it may
be found. Thus in the public life at court there
emerges the idea of political power as a force making
for tragic strife and suffering. Evidently the hero,
Bussy D'Ambois, hoped to rise in the power-world by
truly "honest actions," not by the bogus so-called
"great" deeds which merely mask vice (see I.i.125+--
a key passage on Bussy's heroic optimism).

But Bussy's appointment as "King's Eagle" in the
King's overdue campaign for ridding the court of major
corruption, arouses a swift reaction from the play's
great politic villains, Monsieur and the Duke of Guise
(notorious in then-recent history for his leading part
in the massacre of Protestants at Paris on St. Bartholomew's Day, 1572). They form a coalition to neutralize or, if necessary, to destroy Bussy.

But Acts I-III also dramatize events in the private lives of some prominent people at court. In the
relationship which swiftly flowers between Bussy D'
Ambois and the heroine, Tamyra, Countess of Montsurry,
Chapman sensitively explores sexual power as a force
for joy or suffering in modern society. Thus rises
the issue of personal happiness.

As Act IV begins, these two major structural
themes (the search for public justice against would-
be tyranny; the search for personal happiness) fuse
in the play's action. From then on, they interwork
dynamically to the end. During Acts IV-V the burden
of representing active tyranny is transferred by the
villains to their dupe and tool of murder, Montsurry,
who in the last act emerges as a very strong character during and after the singular torture-scene
(V.i).

A critically important element in the structural design is the imagined time scheme. All the events set before us fall in firmly linked sequences on two consecutive days and nights. Through this time plan Chapman seems to suggest that the forces which generate suffering in modern society appear when passion and reason meet, with their intense conflicts compressed to the utmost in time. Symbolically, time and passion become great powers, almost characters, in the tragedy. The structurally central Bussy-Tamyra love relationship (in the 1607 play she takes more obvious initiative than he does; whereas the 1641 text, mainly visible in *Tragedy*, makes corny melodrama of the love-affair) suggests that, in strong, even relatively decent and honest men and women, passion may rise from below consciousness to rule or overwhelm reason.

Chapman long anticipated such analysts as Freud in his perception of the force of sexuality in society. And his tragic vision incorporates the passion's-storm theme into the dramatic structure, which does indeed yield the "sense that [the lovers'] coming together is a dark but deep compulsion far removed from the ordinary life of the shallow or beastly courtiers" (Ure). Closely held and sustained within a carefully built dramatic structure, Chapman's tragic vision transcends the tidy formulations of systematic moralists (e.g., Ornstein in *The Moral Vision of Jacobean Tragedy*).

Chapman's idea of a tragic hero, Bussy D'Ambois, has aroused criticism which has been sadly muddled by failure of virtually all critics before Brooke to distinguish adequately between two different plays, *Bussy I* (printed 1607) and *Bussy II* (1641; see title-page in O.S.). Since George Chapman knew Christopher Marlowe and recognized his genius, many critics of *Bussy II* are bemused with the fixed idea that Chapman meant slavishly to imitate Marlowe (1) by taking Tamburlaine as the pattern for Bussy D'Ambois as a tragic hero and (2) by imitating (but allegedly without success) *Doctor Faustus* in use of the supernatural. Here is a neat summation, which is ingenious but does *not* apply to the original *Bussy D'Ambois* play, only at best to the posthumous 1641 affair of the same title:

> While Tamburlaine scourges kingdoms with his conquering sword, Bussy [1641] domineers over a peculiarly ignoble group of courtiers and is assassinated by the husband of the lady he has seduced. The earth-shaking vaunts of *Tamburlaine* and the occult agencies of *Dr. Faustus* often seem absurd in Bussy [II].... (Tucker Brooke)

And *Bussy II* criticism repeats over and over the notion that Chapman intended his hero to be a "Marlovian superman" or "titan."

I strongly suggest that, for the original *Bussy D'Ambois*, in major respects Chapman was not intent upon realizing either a form of the Marlovian superman or the so-called "perfect" man, this last allegedly a man who might have been at home in the mythical Golden Age but was grotesquely out of place in a recognizable modern court, most of whose characters are very much "fallen" men and women. (The "perfect" man thesis is ridden by I. Ribner, *Jacobean Tragedy*).

To me, Marlowe's epic figure of Tamburlaine is an exotic evocation of events long past and, to Marlowe, apparently romantic. By contrast, in *Bussy I*, Chapman represents, and very refreshingly too, a credible modern court society, with mixtures of well-observed good and evil embodied in its men and women, who are all as visibly engaged in a pursuit of happiness as most men seem to be today.

Actually, as a hero, Bussy D'Ambois does not go in for Tamburlainian "earthshaking" vaunts at all. His highly energetic and picturesque powers of language, which in Chapman as in Marlowe become a form of symbolic action in this non-naturalistic theatre, are used to pinpoint, satirize, and expose localized corruption and potential tyranny. No superman or "perfect man," Bussy's very human frailties are strongly marked, nowhere more powerfully than by himself in his own very sensitive death speech (V.iii.123-193; pp. 136-140 in Brooke's ed.; radicaly altered in meaning by the 1641 play's melodramatics in the last act, this speech appears in *Tragedy*, ed. O-S., V.iv.76-145; pp. 113-114.)

What about the hero's alleged domineering over "peculiarly" rotten courtiers? Closer analysis of *Bussy I* suggests that Chapman drew close and meaningful distinctions where nobility is concerned. One of these, often overlooked, is the distinction between comic and tragic hypocrisy. We find tragic hypocrisy represented in the heroine Tamyra. But comic hypocrisy appears in such common creatures of the court as the brightly rotten Duchess of Guise, backed up by Beaupre, both of whom, as their bawdy humor suggests, enjoy sexual corruption-as-usual.

In Chapman's original *Bussy*, the hero subtly or strongly satirizes such common and degraded courtiers. Yet he respects and comes to love, "honestly," Tamyra, who is not shown to be sexually vicious. Like Nicholas Brooke, I see no value in rehearsing the "crudities of moral indignation that have been urged against Tamyra (hardly tolerable anyhow when Freud is every man's familiar"). Furthermore, the fallacious notion of Bussy as an intended superman takes no account of the refreshingly down-to-earth human scale and proportion of the Tamyra-Bussy love affair. For therein, with a sensitive psychological realism, Chapman shows how two strong people, seeking happiness in a world whose commonplace corruption they never made, may at least temporarily be subject to an overwhelming passions' storm of sexual love.

As for use of the supernatural, something found in many Renaissance tragedies including Shakespeare's, there is no point whatever in abusing Chapman for not providing for his summoned spirits the kind of spectacular language which Marlowe invented for his Mephistophilis in *Dr. Faustus*. In *Bussy I* (IV.ii. 18-138) one Friar Comolet calls up a spirit, Behemoth, in an effort to secure information on the plots of the villains and their dupe, Montsurry, against D'Ambois and the heroine Tamyra. A bit later on (V.ii.45-67) D'Ambois himself recalls the spirit to get clearer information, if possible.

We suggest that Marlowe's Mephistophilis and Chapman's Behemoth have obviously different dramatic purposes. Just as they differ obviously as "characters." In contrast to Marlowe's mighty devil-figure, Behemoth has very limited knowledge and even less power. Indeed in the first *Bussy* play, he and his aides are not identified as "devils" at all, only as "spirits." Dramatically, Behemoth functions as a sort of spirit-intelligencer, a kind of "private eye" in today's detective-story slang. As such, the effect of his limited powers is to enforce a humanist tragic concept that the fate of men depends decisively upon men and, with this, the idea that modern man is his own worst enemy. Chapman has simply no need for Mephistophilis' poetic mode.

The really meaningful question is: what is the value of the spirit spectacle to the play? We suggest that in our twentieth-century non-naturalistic theatre, given an intelligent production, the spirit spectacle could work very well. Look at IV.ii.80-127 (Brooke's ed., pp. 105-7; in *Tragedy* = IV.ii.101-148; pp. 105-6), Bussy, Tamyra, and Friar Comolet can see but not hear the actions dramatized--the effect is like looking at a television without the sound. Of course the audience sees all and hears all, with the result that we instantly sense the irony and deadly danger of the lovers' developing situation as it moves toward a catastrophe for which the spirit-spectacle helps to prepare us. Anyone keen to compare Shakespeare's handling

of comparable effects may look at *Hamlet*, III.iv.
103-137, where Hamlet sees and hears the Ghost, while
Queen Gertrude directly hears and sees nothing of
her late husband's spirit. If anything, we suggest
that the *Hamlet* ghost is the more melodramatic; for
instance, its reappearance is not dramatically pre-
pared-for but has a jack-in-the-box surprise effect.

Nevertheless, the Chapman of the original *Bussy
D'Ambois* does perhaps owe something to Marlowe, something vital to a tragic sense of life today. "What
distinguishes Chapman and what made it possible for
him to write his masterpiece in tragedy is a fiery and
imaginative response to 'greatness' and its role among
men" (Ure). Some critics, perhaps bedazzled by either
Marlowe's or Shakespeare's tragic preoccupation with
supreme power or with 'right' kingship, are baffled
that Chapman's Bussy has no "ambition to achieve an
earthly crown." Rather his desire is to live through
actions which are not phonily great but individually
honest.

Through his tragic design, Chapman suggests that
in modern society there may be other work for authentic great men than laboring to gain power over others
or to achieve earthly crowns. Coming into view here
is a form of tragedy in which the hero strives with
all his powers to aid justice, to defeat would-be
tyranny, and to achieve happiness through shared love.
Such a concept of a tragic hero and his problems may
have value both for the Renaissance and for our own
time.

Chapman's tragic vision in the first *Bussy* play
is further expressed through the strongly-controlled
plot-structure. Virtually no element in the dramatic
action is left to chance or Fortune. Rather the entire tragic design is rooted in character skilfully
revealed by actions which spring from the conflicts
of strong personalities. Every major figure (Bussy
D'Ambois, King Henry, Monsieur, Guise, Montsurry;

the heroine Tamyra) encounters a varied succession
of tests or challenges. In Chapman's view of human
nature, character is best shown by the individual's
choice of response from the spectrum of possibilities available at any given dramatic moment, both
as this choice is viewed by the character and as
experienced by the audience, which may wittily see
more choices than the character is able to make out
as really available.

This challenge-and-response pattern and dramatic
method for probing the depths of human nature is distinctive of the treatment accorded the major *tragic*
figures. We can illustrate the pattern, ironically
enough, from one who has been mocked (by Muir, for
Bussy II) as a dramatic nobody, mere "cardboard,"
allegedly one of the "minuses whose very names seem
unreal." This is the heroine's husband, Montsurry.

Close reading of the original *Bussy D'Ambois* results in a different view. During the first three
acts Montsurry appears as a mere sycophant and toady
for the "great" would-be tyrants, Guise and Monsieur.
But during Act IV and above all in Act V he emerges
as a figure of strong and even frightening proportions, when he joyously tortures his wife, Tamyra,
and seeks onstage to carve her into an image of all
adultery. Before the tragedy's final phase, I find
no less than nine major tests which the action is designed to present to him.

Here I cite only the final challenge, which comes
during the anguished drama of love against hate after
D'Ambois' death. The ghost of Friar Comolet urges
Montsurry to achieve forgiveness and "Christian re-
concilement" with Tamyra. The audience can sense that
such a truly heroic achievement may be possible if
Montsurry can summon up sufficiently daring and imaginative powers of creative love. Instead, self-
persuaded that he is virtually without human frailty,
and self-enslaved by curiously rigid and contradictory ideas of honor, he shows in his remarkable final

127

speech how he chooses symbolic suicide (V.iii.159-264, ed. Brooke).

Not all the major figures, however, range in the tragic side of life, that is in the side in which men and women dare to encounter serious man-made suffering. The finely drawn villain, Monsieur, and his no. 1 aide, the brutal Guise, show a coldly cynical viciousness controlled by prudent *amour-propre*. Such self-love, highly credible in them, marks those who risk little or nothing. Moved by no ideal higher than self-interest, they belong to what we here term the "comic." Our comment upon the challenge-and-response mode of characterization does not wholly fit them, for their responses are as predictable as corrupt. The Duchess of Guise and her friend Beaupré, among the play's women, share the same cynicism, which we have suggested to be part of comic hypocrisy.

But in striking contrast, Bussy, Tamyra, and Montsurry toward the play's end, meeting life's challenges, respond in ways which ensure suffering and define its meaning. As an observer of human nature under stress, Chapman is most subtle and original, as well as nearest in sympathy to our own age, when he invents dramatic means to show how passions may arise from below consciousness to affect the course of the action decisively.

Indeed, this poignant understanding of the complexities of the passion-reason conflicts in men distinguishes the Chapman of *Bussy I*. Even in the inferior 1641 play it accounts for the "double vision of its hero" (Ure). What this kind of vision signifies is the perhaps permanent tragic dualism generated between man and society (a far-reaching insight first seen strongly working in Marlowe's work, such as *Dr. Faustus*). Not only the hero but Tamyra and Montsurry as well are shown to the audience by means of this "double vision," for they are no less tragically ambiguous. Through this kind of vision we can better understand how it is that strong men and women, who seek happiness through actions which are "honest" to them, and meaningful to us, may ironically effect their own destruction.

The play's leading men offer a rather fascinating gallery of dramatic portraits, drawn from modern power-politics. Although Chapman worked up materials from very recent French history, he did so with imaginative freedom. The historic original of King Henry actually exhibited "a strange compound of sensualism, superstition, cowardice, and ferocity" (Parrott). Chapman's King Henry, however, is his own invention, one designed to fit the purposes of his own plot-structure, no mere stock type either of a dummy or "stock" King who mouths royal sentiments but never acts on them. Examine the first *Bussy D'Ambois* and you will find a King who is dry, sharp, shrewd, witty, resourceful politically, and tough-mindedly just.

As for Monsieur's portrait in *Bussy I*, it far surpasses in wit and depth any mere type of the "ambitious and villainous intriguer" (Parrott) or the stock "satanic Machiavel" (Ornstein). For his brilliant villain, Chapman invented a singularly cruel, obscene wit and humor. Close scrutiny of the dialogue's undermeanings and entendres reveals the powerful "stench of corruption" and "perverse appetite" (Brooke) characteristic of him. His attempted seduction of Tamyra (ed. Brooke II.ii.50-111; most of it is in *Tragedies*, ed. Ornstein-Spencer, II.ii.50-111; p. 88) is explicable as illustrating his vicious humor and sexuality, for she has by then appeared as the *only* decent woman in the court circle!

But when the subtleties of Monsieur's witty speech go unobserved, much of the intended characterization is lost to sight. The brilliant fifth-act exchange of wit between Monsieur and Guise, on the imminent murder of the hero illustrates the point (V.iii.1-55).

This cheerful interchange between the two villains should be read "in character." Then it seems that when they--the very men who have skilfully engineered the plan for D'Ambois' murder from ambush by gangsters--appear to discuss the coming atrocity, they come as supervisors who wish to check up on and enjoy their handiwork. From the audience's viewpoint, therefore, they play a psychologically active role until the hero's death, when, in the original play's staging, they probably left the stage "above." Their witty talk of "Nature" as being to blame for the outrage is, I think, a fantastic piece of their obscene humor.

That Chapman mastered a psychological realism which is meaningful in twentieth-century terms appears, we suggest, in the character of his heroine, Tamyra. (Those who know *Hamlet* may enjoy contrasting the vividness of Tamyra with the relatively pallid and dubiously motivated Ophelia and Gertrude, for we suggest that the last two take on almost all their color by association with their men, whereas their own inner emotional life remains largely lost in dramatic fog).

Even critics of *Bussy II* have long been at odds as to why Tamyra's love-affair with the hero was made so important in the tragic design, an importance even clearer in *Bussy I*. Some have claimed that the heroine's struggle against sexual passion is too brief to be credible. Actually, in *Bussy I*, this problem is paralleled by that of the matching suddenness of Bussy's response and, even more strikingly, by that of the speed with which the heroine's husband, Montsurry, gives way to an outbreak of pathological jealousy which results in his torturing his wife in V.i. In one critic's view (Craig's), the suddenness of the passion and the sequent action by which Tamyra and Bussy become lovers must seem incredible today; while historically Craig falls flatly back upon the notion that Chapman must have swallowed whole one of the traditional Elizabethan ideas about women's "nature," that is, that for a woman to be tempted sexually is for her to fall.

As it happens, only the original *Bussy D'Ambois* (written 1600-1604, or about when Shakespeare was beginning to deal seriously with deep sexuality, in *Hamlet* to *Othello*) contains key passages which illuminate the heroine's inner emotional life (e.g., II.ii. 1-50; ed. O-S. sticks this into the 1641 play-text [p. 87]). Secondly, what is of crucial importance for Tamyra is that the thrust of passion which overwhelms reason and the conventional protective wisdom (social restraints, official morality and vows, piety, custom, etc.) comes from within the depths of her personality or from that mysterious region which today we should term subconsciousness.

Look acutely at the discoveries she makes during the aside and soliloquy at II.ii.145-178; (this is in ed. O-S, II.ii.145-182; pp. 89-90). We see that, in *Bussy I*, the heroine actually takes a degree of initiative toward the hero, after an eruption of desire she cannot restrain at that time. After the investigations of Freud and many others, it has, we think, been sufficiently well established that everyone, no matter how seemingly secure and reasonable (like the Tamyra of *Bussy I*, whose marriage seems happy until we watch her husband, Montsurry, complacently counsel her to "bear with" Monsieur's sexual assaults (II.ii. 113-131; ed. O-S, II.ii.113-131; p. 89), has breaking points where social defenses and self-controls may give way.

In *Bussy I* the instant when reason crumbles before the drive of passion is the moment of highest poetic, theatrical, and human interest. There is nothing necessarily incredible (as Craig blandly thought) in such an event following but "one recorded struggle." (For the Queen in *Hamlet*, we never even hear of one!) For there is no way surely to know

131

how many struggles went unnoticed because their signs
were ambiguous or obscure. For instance, Montsurry
(II.ii.1-33; inserted by ed. O-S, p. 87) is too ob-
tuse to perceive indications of growing passionate
turmoil in his wife, although the more acutely ob-
servant Beaupre does see them and enables the audience to do so as well, with her ironically amused

> I'll leave you Madam to your passions.
> I see, there's change of weather in your looks.

In his masterpiece, the original *Bussy D'Ambois*, Chapman is master of a very powerful form of psychological
realism, one well able to move us today to look sensitively into the mysteries of our own humanity.

We have suggested various ways in which the tragic
vision expressed in the first *Bussy D'Ambois* conveys
ideas about human suffering that are still important.
Even more modern in his outlook than was Christopher
Marlowe, Chapman shows his keen insight into human
nature, into practical morality, and into the workings
of evil in society. Some would-be philosophers today
have tried to prove that Bussy was intended to be seen
as almost the literal embodiment of Golden Age man or
"natural man" (e.g., Ribner). These critics point to
the cynical talk of the villains (V.iii.1-56), who
think "Nature" a botcher; and even more point to King
Henry's strong praise of D'Ambois after forcefully
arresting the second Bussy-Guise quarrel (III.ii.90-
110; in ed. O-S, III.ii.88-107, p. 94).

Does the King see Bussy as the heroic reincarna-
tion of Golden-Age man? We suggest that within the
dynamic structure of the whole action this praise is
both subtly "in character" for Henry and works as
part of his adroit struggle to expose and neutralize
the play's bogus great men and would-be tyrants, Guise
and Monsieur. I know of no evidence that a 1600-1604
London audience expected or craved the literal return
of the mythical Golden Age any more than we do today.

But an excellent point has been made concerning the effect of King Henry's praise of the hero: Bussy D'Ambois is an "unfallen" man "among the fallen," but his "virtues are not [the Biblical] Adam's"; he is "not equipped with innocence, but with native noblesse, spirit and state, genius and an ingenuous soul, the virtues of the Renaissance" (Muir).

This last qualification is of notable force. At least partly, it embodies an idea of a humanist tragic hero which may still have validity. I myself suggest that, in his original *Bussy*, Chapman represents his own individualized ideal of an active courtier, soldier, and scholar, perhaps to be contrasted with Hamlet's introspective inactivism. Finally, this ideal of a modern heroic man is firmly anchored into a strongly coherent dramatic structure.

X   "Dear Beauteous Death, the Jewel of the Just"

John Webster, *The White Devil** (1611-12)

The Elizabethan Tragic Sense of Life to About 1600

Let us first offer a brief retrospect on the
major patterns of Elizabethan drama since Kyd's pioneering *Spanish Tragedy* of *ca.* 1585. Ellis-Fermor

---

*Some tragedies of comparable power and appeal are:

Middleton and Rowley. *The Changeling.*

John Webster. *The Duchess of Malfi.*

(both found in *Tragedy*)

For *The Changeling*, the best edition, with a valu-
able critique, is by N. W. Bawcutt in 'The Revels
Plays' (Cambridge, Mass.: Harvard University
Press, [1958]).

Suggested criticism:

The Complete Works of John Webster. ed. F. L.
Lucas. 4 vols. Chatto & Windus, 1927. (Very
solid historical introductions.)

Travis Bogard. *The Tragic Satire of John
Webster.* U. of Calif., 1955.

Clifford Leech. *John Webster: A Critical Study.*
Hogarth, 1951.

Clifford Leech. *Webster: The Duchess of Malfi.*
E. Arnold, 1963.

(*The Jacobean Drama*) provides a broad view of the
spirit of the 1590s as reflected in its plays. First,
there was a cluster of dramas gratifying the "imper-
ishable instinct for horrors that chill the blood and
raise the hair." But these did not so much really
represent the "average effect of Elizabethan daily
life" as they revealed a "hearty, credulous love of
straightforward bloodshed, murder, and mutilation."
This group includes *The Spanish Tragedy*, Peele's
Battle of Alcazar, Marlowe's *Jew of Malta* and his
Massacre at Paris.

A second cluster of "history" plays--a specialty
of the 1590s--mainly dramatized the robust new patriot-
ism which took on added vigor after the seemingly miraculous defeat of the Spanish Armada in 1588. These
plays celebrate the romantic-heroic story of England's
rise from the world of medieval feudalism to the Tudor
age, with Queen Elizabeth's glorious reign seen as the
superb climax. Dramatically uneven and spotty, these
history plays nevertheless sharpened the playgoing
citizens' keen interest in domestic and foreign politics. Problems of government are explored : the nature
of kingship, good and tyrannous; the character of an
ideal ruler; the state's evolution as common men could
imagine it. Shakespeare's long series is most notable,
but Peele and Greene work this vein, as well as the
Marlowe of *Edward II*.

The special charm of a third cluster, which deals
with fantasy and romance, is exactly their artful lack
of ordinary reality. This group includes, for instance, John Lyly's sophisticated little plays on
mythical subjects, like *Endimion*; Peele's playful *Old
Wives' Tale*; Greene's straightforward tenderness in
Friar Bacon and Friar Bungay; a whole string of early
Shakespearean romantic work (*Love's Labour's Lost*,
Two Gentlemen of Verona, *Midsummer Night's Dream*,
Merchant of Venice); and Dekker's rollicking *Shoemakers' Holiday* (1599). In a fourth group we might
place occasional farces. For instance, the old *Shrew*

play antedating Shakespeare's *Taming of the Shrew*; his own *Comedy of Errors* (based on Plautus). But considering the earlier popularity of English rough-and-tumble farce, its decline in the 1590s is itself a striking phenomenon indicating how tastes change.

Lastly there is a cluster of pioneering tragedies. Kyd and, even more, Marlowe, are the powerful leaders. Tentatively with Kyd, unmistakably with Marlowe's *Tamburlaine* and *Dr. Faustus*, we first get a whole unified world of insights into the human condition worthy to be called a "tragic vision." Marlowe's protagonists all aspire greatly, but in the end they are destroyed by conflict with a universe in which man proceeds at his own peril. In the Marlovian world-view there are no miracles, no kindly interventions of divine providence, no guides (as with Dante in the *Divine Comedy*) capable of leading man to an earthly or heavenly paradise.

The full impact of Marlowe's trailblazing work appears around and after 1600. During the 1590s, Shakespeare first explored tragedy, tentatively, in *Richard III, Romeo and Juliet,* and *Richard II.*

But the general late Elizabethan mood, to about 1598, Ellis-Fermor characterizes as one of triumph. Life is viewed with gusto, even with romantic optimism. Broadly prevalent she finds an expansive and elated spirit. Recurrent dramatic themes confirm belief in the nobleness of man and express delight in human vitality and beauty. The overall tone of the drama seems brilliant, bright, and optimistic of prosperity and national happiness. Such is the heyday of the late Elizabethan drama before the turn of the century toward more corrosive comedy and deeper tragedy.

Changes in the Tragic Sense of Life,

ca. 1600 and After:

Optimism and Pessimism

Beginning roughly around 1600, however, profound changes in the tragic sense of life begin to show. Few or none escaped them. Ribner (*Jacobean Tragedy: The Quest for Moral Order*) suggests boldly that in its overall projected vision of "man's relation to his universe," the new developments have two grand designs or patterns.

For a time, at least, the arch-conservatives, primarily Heywood and Shakespeare--at least through *Hamlet* to *Othello* (1600-1604)--were able to hold fairly strongly and clearly to a "view of the universe as the harmonious creation of an ever-loving God, the parts of the creation observing order and degree, with every element enjoying its proper function as part of the divine plan. Man was at the centre of the universe, the noblest work of God, his life guided and controlled by the power of divine providence." Evil (discernible causes of man-made suffering) was, to these conservatives, "real and active." But as they dramatized its workings, "the means of overcoming evil are always available to man." To them, "the movement of the cosmos was toward a constant rebirth of good out of evil."

Thus the ends of their tragedies can be and typically are "reconciliations." The "forces of evil" have "wrought horror" but have been "at least temporarily vanquished" (Ribner, pp. 1-2). Thus, above all in Shakespeare, we see the persistent power "of the optimistic Christian humanism of the early Renaissance which stressed always the dignity of man and the providence of God." The typical Shakespearean tragic representation of the perpetual battle of man "against the forces of evil in the world" leads to reaffirmation of "order and design in the universe." (I would

go a bit less far than Ribner; to me, *King Lear* offers
no final reconciliation such as Ribner finds.)

Shakespeare, therefore, seems mightily to continue, as long as possible, the ironic but still
humanistically optimistic view of the human condition
first notably dramatized by Thomas Kyd in *The Spanish
Tragedy*. Therein we saw how needless suffering was
generated by the desires of proud, ambitious, resourceful and ruthless men (Lorenzo, Balthasar). In
the midst of a civilized court-society, they create
horror and havoc. But dramatized counter-forces rise
to seek justice and in the end to destroy the evil-
doers. The heroine Bel-Imperia and, most of all,
Hieronimo, do in the end destroy the criminals still
surviving in Act V. Justice has been done. *Hamlet*
and *Othello* still show the Kydian pattern: wrongdoers
are eventually overcome by the proponents of justice,
albeit at dreadful cost.

Apart from these two famous conservatives, however, the dominant mood of Jacobean tragedy takes up
and develops Marlovian dramatic skepticism on the
order and perfection of the universe and on man's
place in it. Ellis-Fermor thought that Marlowe, with
Dr. Faustus the climax, dramatized a "steadily increasing sense of human limitations" and created a
"tone of human defeat," an eventual "mood of spiritual
despair." This last Ellis-Fermor thought one result
of Marlowe's "continuing exploration of the political
system of...Machiavelli" (*Jacobean Drama*).

Ribner also (if we make necessary qualifications)
offers a master view of Jacobean tragedy worth considering. He finds that, apart from Shakespeare, the
major English Renaissance tragedians, from Chapman's
Bussy on [his *Bussy* critique is of the 1641 play],
work from the assumption that the modern world around
them was degenerate and decaying, so that in it "virtue is incapable of survival." Bussy's tragedy, from
his viewpoint, is that of a man who, drawn into the
corrupt court world, hopes and intends to keep his own

integrity and believes it within his power to do so.
Ironically, as he takes part in that court world, it
proves impossible not to become, in some significant
measure, corrupted.

To Ribner, Bussy's "tragedy is the tragedy of
all of us who must live in a world where such virtues
[as Bussy's initial integrity and honesty] can no
longer exist" (7). Chapman's central theme is said
to be "the inability of justice to survive in a vitiated world" (7). The only hope Ribner sees for
Chapman's heroes is that they may be able to hold
out, against the "corroding force of the world,"
personal stamina drawn from stoicism and its ideals
of what it is "to be a man."

In Ribner's view the "drive" that produced Chapman's finest work is also illustrated in the best of
such varied tragic writers as Tourneur, Webster,
Middleton, and Ford. Each in his own way, they were
all struggling "to find a basis for morality [that is,
a way to answer the ancient problem of evil, to find
adequate causes for needless suffering] in a world in
which the traditional bases no longer seem to have
validity." They seem to ask: if the world "seems to
give reason only for despair," what kind of "affirma-
tion" of life, what "meaning in human suffering," can
be found? (Ribner 7-8). The upshot was, to Ribner,
a tragic "pessimism" that also links the Jacobean age
to our own 20th-century "age of anxiety." There is
some usable wisdom in all these ideas.

Some Qualifications and a Positive View:

We wish, however, to suggest some qualifications,
even while recognizing the acuteness and modern relevance of the views just summarized. First, we strongly
hold that many of the best writers, from Chapman to
Ford, develop a relatively new and modern kind of
heroism. We find in Chapman's original characteriza-

tion of Bussy D'Ambois a fascinating kind of tragic hero, an image of credible human greatness which finds new work to do in modern society. This work is to strive for justice, to seek defeat of would-be tyranny, and to search for happiness through shared love. A kind of epic grandeur and romantic over-sizing of the tragic heroes (distinctly a tendency in Marlowe and, in different ways, in much of Shakespeare) gives way to a heroism more human in its scale and proportions, more down-to-earth, less remote from the broad ranges of human experience.

Secondly, this newer heroism is exactly drama-tized *in and through* these complex strivings. The heroes do not *begin* in a condition of near despair (as many do in 20th-century tragic drama; e.g., in many of Beckett's pieces, from *Waiting for Godot* on). Eventual defeat and destruction is, in all tragedy, the common lot of the protagonists. If these defeats and this destruction are to move us deeply, what is striven for must in some sense appear to us still pro-foundly worth the effort and even the dreadful cost.

Thomas Kyd's *Spanish Tragedy* for instance, is usually said to have touched off a whole series of "revenge plays," of which *Hamlet* is now the most famous (see F. Bowers, *Elizabethan Revenge Tragedy*). In my view, these are plays not simply of revenge but of something much more durably significant for human dignity, namely a *search for justice*. Of course as long as men firmly felt that the entire universe, as in the typical medieval world-view, was governed by divine Providence and therefore divine justice, such a human search as 17th-century Renaissance tragedies often represent is one thing. Hence the Middle Ages could have their grand "comedy of evil."

But certainly the critical analyses of man and society which the serious drama undertakes, at least by Chapman's first *Bussy D'Ambois*, does *not* wholly encourage or much sustain the old humanist optimism

noted by Ellis-Fermor. On the other hand, neither
is there, I think, quite as clear a case as Ribner
seeks to make for the idea that meaningful human virtues "can no longer exist" or "justice survive in a
vitiated world."

Rather, we think, when it becomes clearer, as it
did to such tragedians as Chapman, Webster, and Ford,
that modern man is his own worst enemy, that man is
wolf to man, and that men can create their own hells
while they live on earth, then the grand result is a
remarkable and 'modern' clarification of the tragic
sense of life, or the meaning of being human, of the
meaning of human dignity and justice. Our earlier
sketch of the English tragic spirit and of English
concepts of a tragic hero indicated, crucially, that
from as early as old *Beowulf*, Englishmen seem rarely
to have expected an easy time of it in this world.
From early times, they delighted in a terrific fight
against long odds. When things looked hopeless,
their heroic spirits show frequent releases of new
creative energies.

We think that Mr. Ribner, with an excess of
20th-century depressive sentimentalism, offers several fallacious *implied* ideas: that if the hero
cannot survive or does not survive his encounter
with active evil, then "virtue" and "justice" cannot
survive either, or cannot even *revive*. Hence the
hero's struggles were in effect absurd, and he was
some kind of a fool, to begin with. (Why didn't the
chap have the common-sense to realize he was beaten
before making a move? and so play it cool, retreat
from the confrontation with evil, swallow the requisite degree and kind of spiritual or other degradations, and live a while longer?)

Nothing whatever is proved by the mere fact that
tragic heroes die. In the long run, we all do. This
is merely a commonplace fact of life, proving nothing.
The relevant question is--and this *is* sensitively ex-

plored by Chapman, Webster, Middleton, and Ford--what
is the meaning of life when the heroes and heroines
make willing sacrifices for goals we can sympathize
with as worth the struggle?

If, as Ribner notes, many traditional bases for
morality no longer, after about 1600, seemed to many
tragic writers to have validity in their inward essence, not outward shows or appearance, then--we sug-
gest--the problem, for some, emerges as this: how to
find better bases of morality which *are* more adequate
to the needs and society of modern man?

Furthermore, the world as dramatized by the best
minds of the Renaissance (including at least *King
Lear* for Shakespeare) is far from "vitiated," as we
see it. Some crucial insights derive from the 'new'
tragedy of reason versus passion, of which Chapman was
the pioneer. For one thing, as tragic hero, Bussy
D'Ambois is challenged to and does oppose active evil
(Monsieur, Guise) with active, creative, and positive
forces for what he believes to be good, both public
and personal. Secondly, the forces dramatized as decisive for the hero and heroine are shown to be by no
means wholly rational. Rather they represent deep
drives stemming from what today we call the subcon-
scious part of total personality.

Thirdly, the counter-responses of the dramatized
forces of evil begin, by *Bussy D'Ambois*--this is even
more profoundly worked into the tragic vision in
Webster's *White Devil*--to take on a remarkably enlarged destructive vitality. The new kinds of villains no longer stop when something like a limited
and specific triumph, rational or Machiavellian, has
been achieved. Rather they seem inclined to widen out
the range of their endeavors, as though to obliterate
all possible good in the world, to "make a desert and
call it peace." This famous phrase was used long ago
by critics of the ancient Roman campaign to subjugate
primitive England. (The tragic parallel may be clearer

142

if one realizes that this England was once viewed
somewhat as North Vietnam seems to have been in
much official U.S. policy in 1968, not to speak of
the men who dreamt of "victory" by annihilation
"back to the Stone Age.")

This evil delight in spreading human outrage
widely may be seen in the last act of the original
Bussy D'Ambois, after the top villains have transferred the burden of the action against the hero to
Montsurry. Montsurry proceeds to "make a desert and
call it peace": his wild, demented torture of Tamyra
(all in the name of "honor") and the foul murder of
D'Ambois result, for Montsurry, in a pyrrhic triumph.
For in the name of victory, he has succeeded, ironically, in destroying everything that has made life
worth living for him and for Tamyra.

On Webster's Own Tragic Art

Webster's strange, non-naturalistic art, whose
haunting or nightmare power even his critical enemies
hardly dare deny, has been gradually winning new ad-
herents in the middle and later 20th-century. Perhaps we have learned something about the human capa-
cities for evil and enormous destruction from two
World Wars and their sequels, in this century which
has been termed, without undue exaggeration, one of
"total war." To Victorians and even to such a comfortable rationalist as George Bernard Shaw, Webster's
vision of evil triumphant was counter to their whole
belief that progress, both technological and moral,
was proceeding inseparably and inevitably toward ever-
higher plateaus of generally enjoyed freedom and widespread well-being.

Webster's insights are embodied in two remarkable
tragedies: *The White Devil* (1609-1612) and *The Duchess of Malfi* (1612-1614). Both are better compared,
if Shakespearean comparisons must be made, to *King*

143

Lear rather than to the relatively optimistic *Hamlet*,
Othello, or *Macbeth*. But we quite agree with Ribner
that there is little point in assuming that Shakespearean modes of characterization and drama apply
to Chapman, or to Webster, or to Middleton and Rowley,
or to John Ford (*Jacobean Tragedy*, p. 23).

Webster's plots are derived fairly directly from
16th century Italian history. Indeed, the action of
The White Devil was based on terrible events barely
two decades old, and if anything Webster has softened
rather than accentuated the horrors which actually
took place. Tucker Brooke has some shrewd general observations (*The Renaissance*). While the stage business in Webster recalls Kyd's busy inventiveness,
Webster's "strange art is far more intelligent....His
style is curiously unrhythmic, except in the songs
which crash in like the trumpets of doom, upon the
cacophonies of mundane speech." His death scenes,
in both his best plays, are probably the greatest in
Elizabethan literature; what in a less skilled artist
would become anti-climactic, in Webster "is kept aloft
by (his) mastery of the macabre." His "dialogue is
often patched with sayings from Sidney, Montaigne, or
Donne." [To an audience some of whose members would
more or less recall the wisdom of these rare men, the
effect was to concentrate that wisdom upon the tragic
spectacle of modern man as his own worst enemy].

"His view of life is Elizabethan rather than
Jacobean in the sharp distinction he maintains between good and bad and the straight-forwardness with
which he faces death and horror....He is one of the
most romantic of dramatists. Life, he teaches [or
rather the Duchess of Malfi dramatically perceives]
is a labyrinth." Near the beginning of *Duchess*, the
heroine gravely says to her loyal friend:

> ...I am going into a wilderness,
> Where I shall find nor path nor friendly clue
> To be my guide.

To Brooke, in Webster "The only constant is death, up to which he leads his characters relentlessly, and dismisses them under the glare of death's illumination. He makes no theological assertions, but the reading of him is a kind of religious experience, and if any affinity for him must be sought among the Stuart writers, it will be found in such mystic poets as Herbert and Vaughan." [For they too are profoundly stirred to seek life's greatest meaning at the moment of its going out.]

> Dear, beauteous death, the jewel of the just,
>   Shining nowhere but in the dark,
> What mysteries do lie beyond thy dust,
>   Could man outlook that mark!

> (Vaughan, in "They are all
> gone into the world of light")

The Relevance of Conditions of Civilization to the Sense of Life Dramatized in Webster's Tragic Vision

We suggested earlier that, for the flourishing of tragedy, there must be widely felt a sense of profound moral crisis. The more sensitive men, at least, must perceive the strong likelihood that the traditional "platforms" of value are collapsing under them. That, in the historian Arnold Toynbee's phrase, civilization has entered upon a prolonged "time of trouble," when its very survival is in doubt. Such a feeling was evidently widespread among the most cultured men in western Europe by about 1500-1610.

The civilization of Italy, where the Renaissance was already old and decadent, offered to Jacobeans (1603+) most striking evidence that a deeply tragic view of life alone made good sense. It is therefore no accident that so many tragedians drew upon Italian experience for large-scale metaphors for this view. In this brief account, we have drawn especially upon— and many quotes are from—the still-valuable *Civil-*

145

ization of the Renaissance in Italy by Hermann Burckhardt (Phaidon ed.). Although more recent historians
regard his account as oversimplified, something like
it made sense to such an artist as John Webster.

By the early 16th century (whence came the real-
life source of *The Duchess of Malfi*), Italian civilization had developed a dynamic for destruction and
death so that what might seem (with *Duchess'* or *White
Devil's* plots) like the wild invention of a morbid
writer represented merely an extension of everyday
life. The violent destruction of such people as the
Duchess, her husband Antonio, and their children
(*Duchess of Malfi*); or of the more complex Brachiano
and Vittoria (*White Devil*); was everywhere accepted
as a foregone certainty. By the early 16th-century,
Renaissance civilization had reached in Italy its
zenith.

Simultaneously the breakdown in political and
personal morality was such that many, like Machiavelli,
surmised that the ruin of the nation was inevitable.
"'We Italians are irreligious and corrupt above
others'" (Machiavelli in *Discorsi*). Some thought the
Italians had become so highly individualized as to
have outgrown "natural" limits of religion and morality which sufficed in an earlier, "undeveloped
state." And that Italians widely despised "outward
law, because our rulers are illegitimate [i.e., held
power by violence alone], and their judges and of-
ficers wicked men." On this condition, Machiavelli,
who prided himself not on conventional morality but
on calling spades spades, commented, "'Because the
Church and her representatives set us the worst example." (Consider the greatly wicked Churchmen who
figure so decisively in *Duchess* and *White Devil*).

Many outstanding Italians had in fact, "substi-
tuted for holiness--the Christian idea of life--the
cult of historical greatness" and "glory," or of
"fame." Both glory and fame were often pursued with
"frightful...boundless ambition and thirst...., in-

dependent of all means and consequences." In the preface to his history of Florence, Machiavelli remarks that it is a gross error in historians not to realize that "'many who could distinguish themselves by nothing praiseworthy, strove to do so by infamous deeds!'" Moreover, when considering the actions of men in supreme power, Machiavelli found that "'actions which are great in themselves, as is the case with the actions of rulers and states, always seem to bring more glory than blame, of whatever kind they are and whatever the result of them may be.'"

Many serious writers of the age, when searching for motives, find them above all in the "burning desire to achieve something great and memorable. This ...is not a mere case of ordinary vanity, but something daemonic, involving a surrender of the will, the use of any means, however atrocious, and even an indifference to success itself" (B. 80). *I.e.*, the would-be great evil-doers may become oblivious even to their own survival--a strange irony indeed.

In this light, Machiavelli accounts for several notorious Florentine murders; and other historians back him up. (One of these murderers strikingly resembles the furious Lodovico of *The White Devil*, whose savage "Banish'd!" opens the play.) Thus Machiavelli speaks of a proud Italian who had suffered public mockery. Brooding upon a deed so novel and daring that it would lead men to forget his disgrace, he ended by assassinating his kinsman and prince, Duke Alessandro of Florence, in 1537. Such deeds and motives, in Burckhardt's view, "are characteristic features of this age of overstrained and despairing passions and forces." From the grave moral crisis of its civilization, hardly any of the best men saw escape.

What "bulwark against evil", if any, did these Renaissance men see? Of all moral forces visible to them (records Burckhardt), the "sentiment of honor"

seemed most likely to provide protection. But this
is "that enigmatic mixture of conscience and egotism
which often survives in the modern man after he has
lost, whether by his own fault or not, faith, love,
and hope. This sense of honor is compatible with
much selfishness and great vices, and may be the
victim of astonishing illusions....It is certainly
not always easy, in treating...this period, to distinguish this sense of honor from the passion for
fame, into which, indeed, it easily passes."

Besides, account must be taken--as Webster's
tragedies do--of the highly developed modern imagination which, in the most sophisticated men, "gives to
(their) virtues and vices a peculiar color" so that
"under its influence (their) unbridled egotism [it-
self one result of Renaissance admiration for the
"boundless development of the individual" and his
genius] shows itself in its most terrible shape."
One way this peculiarly heightened imagination appears, in life, as in the tragic drama, is in gambling on a large scale.

Hamlet gambles that the play-within-the-play
will catch the conscience of King Claudius; since
Claudius probably surmises the ordeal prepared for
him, he also gambles on his powers of dissembling.
Brutus gambles that Caesar's assassination will restore health to the republic. King Lear gambles
enormously by irrevocably giving all his power to
his children. Macbeth and his Lady, as gamblers in
this sense, bet everything on their ability to murder
King Duncan, keep it forever secret, then rule be-
nignly which, in Shakespeare's source, they did for
ten years.

In the *Duchess of Malfi*, the Duchess and her
honorable lover Antonio, gamble everything on their
ability to keep their marriage secret. In *The White
Devil*, Brachiano and Vittoria gamble enormously on
their power to frustrate the combined vengeances of

Francisco de Medicis and Cardinal Monticelso; but
their fate is sealed when Monticelso becomes Pope
and throws all his vast powers into their destruction.

The Italian and Renaissance imagination also
found expression in the "peculiar character" of vengeance, which sought to make the revenge a consummate
work of art, when active evil had become a fine art
itself, as it did particularly among the more sophisticated, such as the antagonists in *Duchess of Malfi*
and *White Devil*. But peasants and aristocrats alike
formed the concept that to be truly satisfactory, a
revenge must be artful, "compounded of the material
injury and moral humiliation of the offender. A mere
brutal, clumsy triumph of force was held by public
opinion to be no satisfaction. The whole man, with
his sense of fame and of scorn, not only his fist,
must be victorious" (B, 226-7).

When not themselves corrupt, the government and
its tribunals, with the Church, might officially de-
plore these "perfect" revenges. They could usually
do little more, for both had become powerless, knew
it, and only hoped to keep vengeances within some
limits. Indeed, such a broad historical view of late
Renaissance civilization in Italy showed a world in
which the powers making for death seemed almost everywhere to be triumphant.

Occasionally (notes Burckhardt) one hears of attempted reconciliations. [Compare the occasional
"non-aggression" pacts made between nations in the
20th-century; with a Hitler, these were normal indications of the next target for conquest]. We have
such a reconciliation dramatized in *White Devil*, with
deep irony and ill-concealed hostility (at III.ii.
291-6; *Tragedy*, pp. 142-3). But apparently such
public rituals, often accompanied by solemn protesta-
tions of good will and peace, only briefly restrained
great feuds already in action.

It was widely felt that "'there must be art in the vengeance'". Typically the late-Renaissance Italian (says Burckhardt) "shrank...from no dissimulation in order to attain his ends," just as he was "wholly free from hypocrisy in matters of principle. In these he attempted to deceive neither himself nor others." Dramatically, of course, this may lead to such deeply ironic scenes in *White Devil* as, IV.i (ed. O-S, pp. 146-7), between the two great villains, Francisco de Medicis and Cardinal Monticelso. For differing reasons, both desire the destruction of Brachiano and Vittoria. Each pretends no such foul aim, as each makes gestures of being pious, like Francisco's

> Free me, my innocence, from treacherous acts!
> I know there's thunder yonder [i.e., divine
>   justice to be faced],
>   and I'll stand
> Like a safe valley....

After which, most casually, Francisco says gossip tells him Cardinal Monticelso has a book, kept up-to-date, listing Rome's "notorious offenders." The Cardinal genially produces his "black book" and even lends it, as though piously unaware that Francisco urgently wishes to hire some murderers. In *White Devil*, at this point in the action, *both* want Brachiano and Vittoria murdered; both, adroitly, as artists, intend that the actual crime shall be done by ambitious underlings. Each pretends to the other to be merely frivolous. Neither deceives the other. Both keep in mind, explicitly or implicitly (for Monticelso in this scene; but his hatred of Vittoria and Brachiano has already been established in the play), very vividly, the image of the wrong whose revenge they seek (see Francisco at *Devil*, IV.i.95-99).

In Webster's *The White Devil*, of course, the heroine Vittoria is neither white (in the sense of being morally innocent, even passively so [like the

150

Isabella of Shakespeare's *Measure for Measure* when first we meet her]) nor a devil (in the sense of being guilty of all the heroic rottenness of which Cardinal Monticelso accuses her, in the remarkable trial-scene [III.i]).

What Happens in the Action of 'The White Devil'

The story is based on actual life. In Italy, a quarter of a century before Webster wrote his tragedy, the events of it had made a deep impression. (In our account of them and of the action, we draw freely on *The Works of John Webster*, ed. F. Lucas, I, 70-85). Lucas observes that "the [historical] narrative is of extraordinary interest in itself, and nothing can convey better the siren spell of Renaissance Italy, which fascinated Webster and his audience, and must be felt by the modern reader likewise, before Webster's two great tragedies can produce their full effect."

Here are the outlines of the action in *The White Devil*: The middle-aged Duke of Brachiano falls in love with Vittoria Corombona, wife of the sickly dotard Camillo. This Camillo is nephew of the powerful Cardinal Monticelso, later Pope Paul IV [in history, Sixtus V]. But Brachiano happens to be married to the virtuous Isabella, sister of Duke Francisco de Medicis of Florence. And loathes her, almost in proportion as Vittoria fascinates him. Vittoria's ambitious and ruthlessly Machiavellian brother, Flamineo, arranges to have Isabella poisoned. And Flamineo supervises destroying Camillo by breaking his neck, under cover of a pretended accident. Flamineo's own motive is sheer self-advancement in a dog-eat-dog world; see his savage denunciation of his mother, Cornelia, for being poor and leaving him no alternative than to be miserable or to rise by doing great men's dirty work (I.ii.351-388; in ed. O-S, pp. 128-129).

Indeed his view sharply recalls Bussy D'Ambois
grim observation in Chapman's play (1600-1604) on
what it takes to become rich and powerful in modern
society: "Who is not poor, is monstrous" (I.i.3).

Duke Brachiano is too powerful to be attacked
directly. So his mistress Vittoria is instead brought
to trial, charged with the murder of her husband,
Camillo, and with adultery with Brachiano. The trial
is a brilliant travesty of justice. Vittoria's chief
accusers and judges are her and Brachiano's greatest
enemies, Cardinal Monticelso (uncle of the murdered
Camillo) and Francisco, Duke of Florence (brother of
the murdered Isabella). [Needless to say, the
Medicis were famous for their revenges]. The outcome
of the trial is, first, that Vittoria is condemned to
confinement in a house of Convertites, or penitent
whores. The intent of the accusers of Vittoria was,
at the same time, to discredit Brachiano publicly as
the lover of a known whore.

From this imprisonment, Vittoria is rescued by
Brachiano. In his own strange, tortuous ways, he
seems to love her passionately, as she does him. He
carries her off to Padua, where they are married.
Meanwhile, Cardinal Monticelso is elected Pope Paul
IV [despite all desperate efforts of the historic
Brachiano to prevent this calamity to his interests].

Now the lovers' two powerful enemies, the Pope
and the Duke of Florence, relentlessly resume their
campaign of vengeance. The Pope excommunicates the
lovers. But Duke Francisco resolves on more material
revenge for his poisoned sister Isabella. Aided by
one Lodovico (whose vengeful cry of "Banish'd!" opens
the play), the Duke makes his way in disguise to Padua.
There he and Lodovico, the poisoners, disguise themselves as holy men, Capuchin monks; and they kill
Brachiano by means of a poisoned helmet, with the
intent that he shall die slowly, in utmost agony,
and in full consciousness that he dies without bene-

152

fit of the last rites of the Catholic Church. It
is one of the greatest death-scenes in Renaissance
tragedy, and few last cries can be more horrible
than Brachiano's despairing scream for "Vittoria!
Vittoria!" (V.iii.174; ed. O-S, p. 162).

Vittoria remains alive. Her brother Flamineo,
who casually kills his own virtuous brother Marcello
in a brawl, sees his sister left the Duke Brachiano's
wealthy heiress. He tries to blackmail her. But he
is interrupted by Lodovico & confederates, who complete their and Duke Francisco's vengeance by killing
Vittoria and Flamineo together.

The murderers do not, however, escape. The
young prince, Giovanni Orsini (son and heir of Brachiano by Isabella) leads a posse, wounds Lodovico, and
apprehends him to be brought to justice. Lodovico
proudly boasts that he personally drew or "limn'd this
night piece" and that the fame he will gain by the
enterprise "shall crown it and quit the shame." To
him, it is his masterpiece, as an artist in murder.
Lodovico cheerfully confesses [contrast Iago's refusal to do so at the end of *Othello*] and implicates
Duke Francisco in the murders of Vittoria and Flamineo. Prince Orsini orders Lodovico to execution,
grimly proclaiming

> All that have hands in this
>   shall taste our justice,
> As I hope Heaven.

But the sardonic and brilliant villain Lodovico has
almost the last words in the play, an expression of
triumphant satisfaction:

> I do glory yet
> That I can call this act mine own. For my part,
> The rack, the gallows, and the torturing wheel
> Shall be but sound sleeps to me; here's my rest:
> I limn'd [designed and made] this night-piece,
>   and it was my best.

White Devil, V.vi.195-299 (*Tragedy*, p. 172)

George Bernard Shaw, who never could understand how great passions can rise from below subconsciousness to overwhelm reason, as in the love-affair of Brachiano and Vittoria, did not know Webster's historical accuracy and jeered at him as an inventor of bogies, like the waxwork chamber of horrors at Mme. Tussaud's in London.

If anything, Webster somewhat softened the truth he found in history. (See Lucas' edition, I, 70-85). Lucas sums up the last hours of the real-life Vittoria thus:

> On the Sunday night of December 22nd, 1585, there were high revels in the palazzo where Lodovico had collected half a hundred gentlemen and ruffians of his following. (Wearing fantastic masks, in the winter-evening's darkness, a band of them made their way to the Palazzo dei Cavalli, where Vittoria was living. Two traitors had left the doors open.) Vittoria was at prayer, for it was the eve of Santa Vittoria's Day, and the voice of her younger brother Flamineo [Webster's Marcello], singing the *Miserere* to his lute in the next room, deadened the sound of approaching feet. (Hit by two shots, Flamineo crawled) screaming into his sister's bedroom, pursued by the three chief of Lodovico's ruffians. Vittoria was on her knees before her crucifix. (The boy was stabbed in more than fifty places.) They turned to Vittoria with 'Now you are to receive the reward of your iniquities.' Time to confess was refused her. Then, as their rough hands tore open her dress, she cried, 'I forgive you, but I will die clothed.' While Count Paganello and Splandiamo Adami of Fermo held her,

Toledo Visconti of Recanati plunged his
dagger in her breast and, working it in
the wound, asked her with obscene jests,
'Do I touch your heart?' The victim
moaned, 'Gésu...perdono,' and died.
Struck with a sudden revulsion, Visconti
exclaimed, 'Alas! What have we done?
We have killed a saint!' The assassins
searched the house for valuables, and
departed.

But the assassins were swiftly hunted down and
brought to a public justice. By December 27th, the
verdict came from Venice: "Death within three hours."
When the sentence was read to Lodovico, "it wrung from
him no comment beyond the Stoic Italian 'Pazienza!"
"In all due ceremony he was strangled with a cord of
red silk. Yet, before he died, "he wrote to his young
wife in Venice a fine and generous letter...still
extant,...as one more witness to the incalculable
mixture of qualities in the human heart" (Lucas).

If it is any comfort to the reader, in the after-
math most of the other principal figures in the historic tragedy found "swift and evil ends." When at
long last the revenges for the murdered Francesco
Peretti (the play's Camillo) were complete, the historic Pope Sixtus had Peretti's body taken from its
obscure grave and re-interred, with great pomp, in
the Sistine Chapel of Santa Maria Maggiore in Rome,
where he himself was soon to lie. And as the grimly
resolute old Pope lay dying, Lucas tells us, thunder
rattled above the Quirinal Hill; and the Roman popu-
lace "muttered that it was surely Satan come at last
to carry off the soul that--in return for the Triple
Crown of the Papacy--had been sold him long ago."

Ironically, the play's Giovanni is the historic
Duke Virginio Orsini, who actually visited England
in 1600, was entertained at Queen Elizabeth's court,

155

and just possibly received a Shakespearean compliment
by being put into *Twelfth Night* as the romantically
love-sick Duke Orsino of Illyria, who opens that play
with

> If music be the food of love, play on!
> Give me excess of it that, surfeiting,
> The appetite may sicken, and so die.

Webster could not possibly, then, have made Vittoria's
life-drama more tragic than the truth of history.
What he has done in *The White Devil* is to make it
"immortal by his sheer poetry" (Lucas) and by his
great powers as a dramatist.

XI   John Ford's *The Broken Heart*
              and Ford's Tragic Vision

     This touching play, one of the last tragedies
of real power in the English Renaissance drama, is
not of the heroic world of epic conquests, strivings
for supreme dominion, empire-building or other such
grandscale doings. Rather it dramatizes, almost with
understatement, intensely personal conflicts of love
and honor, which are projected as basic forces oper-
ating within a clearly-defined framework of recogniz-
ably modern society. The placing of the action in a
fictional ancient Sparta is a mere theatrical convenience. The age for which Ford wrote could readily
recognize its own face beneath these fictional trappings.

The Broken Heart, (*ca.* 1625-1633)

Suggested criticism

        Clifford Leech. *John Ford and the Drama of
        His Time.* Chatto and Windus, 1957.

        George Sensabaugh. *The Tragic Muse of John
        Ford.* Stanford, 1944.

        Peter Ure. "Marriage and the Domestic Drama in
        Heywood and Ford," *English Studies*, XXXII (1951),
        200-216.

        The "Revels Plays" edition by T. J. B. Spencer
        (forthcoming in 1973) should supersede earlier
        editions.

The central theme and source of the conflicts is forced marriage. Inseparable from this, in Ford's tragic vision, are the cruel wrongs and spiritual destruction done to admirable human beings when true lovers are separated and when one (here, the woman) is forced into a loveless and wretched union. Obviously all this action takes place in a society in which for all practical purposes divorce is simply non-existent or unattainable.

The central drama is one of singularly sustained pathos. Ford does not try for "heroic" or grant effects; this is not Wagnerian opera à la "Tristan and Isolde." Rather he is concerned to explore suffering in psychological depth.

As basis for a critical overview, here is a brief sketch of what happens in *The Broken Heart*. The major true-lovers are Orgilus and Penthea, drawn as decent souls who wanted no more than to marry and to be let alone thereafter. But her brother Ithocles, who has decisive legal power, acts for what he takes to be her best interests: he coerces his sister into a wealthy marriage with old Bassanes. When the damage to her has been done, Ithocles realizes he has done a foul and monstrous thing. Ironically, he is able to realize as much because by then he has formed a true-love relationship with the good, brave-hearted Calantha, a Spartan princess. Penthea feels married in spirit to her former fiance, Orgilus, but her legal marriage to Bassanes forces her to live in symbolic adultery, a "spotted whore."

When the resulting spiritual degradation becomes unbearable, she loses both all will to live and sanity as well, then starves herself to death (starvation here being not only physical but emotional). Although Penthea's first and true love, Orgilus, has been powerless to prevent her destruction, he can and does revenge her and himself. After a mock-reconciliation with Ithocles, Orgilus kills him. He then gladly accepts a death-sentence, for he too is sick of liv-

ing. He has reached that despairing modern state
of being in which all the traditional answers to the
tragic question, why is there so much needless suffering in the world? have gone dead as cold ashes.
Long after Ford's *The Broken Heart*, Orgilus' final
mood was expressed:

> From too much love of living,
>   From hope and fear set free,
> We thank with brief thanksgiving
>   Whatever gods may be
> That no life lives for ever;
> That dead men rise up never;
> That even the weariest river
>   Winds somewhere safe to sea.

> (Swinburne, "Garden of Proserpine")

He elects death by bleeding, and this is gravely en-
acted on stage. When all others are too horrified to
help, old Bassanes (the dead Penthea's cruel husband)
does so, ironically out of a need to expiate his own
crimes against her spirit. Finally Calantha, her own
will to live broken, dies like a Spartan queen before
us, dies of "a broken heart." As she does so, there
is music and a mourning song which points up this
tragedy of wasted youth:

> ...Youth may revel; yet it must
> Lie down in a bed of dust....
>   Love only reigns in death; though art
> Can find no comfort for a broken heart.

For *The Broken Heart*, no literary plot-source
is known, and we think it idle to speculate on remote
resemblances drawn between Penthea-Bassanes and historically known loveless marriages in Elizabethan
society. We think that Ford has designed a structure
of theme, plot, and character to express his own vision of men and society.

159

It is worthwhile in connection with Ford's vision of a "marriage of true minds" to recall briefly the two main traditional attitudes toward marriage which the Elizabethans inherited from past social history. One such view regarded marriage as the lesser of two evils (as St. Paul did), and necessarily a kind of "war between men and women." Chaucer's Wife of Bath, in her Prologue in the *Canterbury Tales*, racily sums up this durable idea. To her down-to-earth mind, happiness in marriage is only possible when one partner or the other wins the war, imposes unconditional surrender, and is accepted by the defeated partner as undisputed master. (Of course, in her five marriages, the sturdy Wife of Bath always set out to win the war herself. An expert in "the old dance," she tells just how she turned the tricks.)

Secondly, the Elizabethans inherited the idea that romantic love was a reality but that it was (as in medieval romance) normally adulterous. Indeed, traditionally, marriage itself was supposed to cure the partners of romantic love toward each other. (Some of these ideas were discussed earlier in the general introductions to comedy and to tragedy.) As a matter of historical fact, it was two English poets, Edmund Spenser and William Shakespeare, who first attempted (in all Europe, as far as I know) to imagine how marriage and romantic love ("true love") might just possibly be reconciled--a profoundly radical and optimistic idea.

This potential reconciliation is expressed variously in Spenser's very personal sonnet-sequence, "Amoretti," and in the marriage poems he wrote in honor of his bride, such as the lovely "Epithalamion," which was his chief wedding-present as well, since he was too poor to afford the conventional kinds of costly gifts.

The theme of this possible reconciliation becomes, in Shakespeare, that which inquires, in
plays (e.g., *Romeo and Juliet*, and many comedies)
and poems, into the "marriage of true minds," which
fascinated John Ford and is central to *The Broken
Heart*. Here is Shakespeare's sonnet 116, followed
by a plain explication designed to clarify this expression of Elizabethan romantic and marital idealism:

Let me not to the marriage of true minds
Admit impediments. Love is not love
Which alters when it alteration finds,
Or bends with the remover to remove.
O no! it is an ever-fixed mark
That looks on tempests and is never shaken;
It is the star to every wandering bark,
Whose worth's unknown, although his height be taken.
Love's not Time's fool, though rosy lips and cheeks
Within his bending sickle's compass come;
Love alters not with his brief hours and weeks,
But bears it out even to the edge of doom.
    If this be error, and upon me proved,
    I never writ, nor no man ever loved.

    The whole poem deals with what the poet finds to
be "true" love in implicit contrast to what is false,
no matter how it may appear to the conventional-mind-
ed who are duped by the customary shows of things.
The speaker refuses absolutely to admit the validity
of social barriers ("impediments") to the marriage
of "true minds." Implicitly, such "true" minds are
healthy, the opposite are sick, no matter what official morality may say.

    The idealized "marriage of true minds" trans-
cends such moralities. This kind of love is *not* subject to decay, although physical bodies are subject
to the erosions of time. The speaker images positive-
ly this kind of love through the metaphor of a firmly-

161

fixed navigational mark, or a star mariners can
safely steer by through all storms. Time may play
harsh jokes (again, by bringing, with age, decay to
"rosy lips and cheeks"), for Time has power over
physical youth. But such youth and its beauty is
not the heart of the matter. Over the spiritual
bond that links true lovers, Time has no power; and
true love can last through life, with a hint of outlasting death, almost to doomsday ("edge of doom").
So much by way of explication of Shakespeare's memorable sonnet.

Hazelton Spencer, in a brief critique, finds
Ford's tragic vision notable on six counts: that he
is "generous and romantic" in spirit; that he is
always deeply moved by lovers' trials; that he is a
poet for whom "the spiritual union of lovers is an
inviolable thing, and wedlock adulterous without a
marriage of true minds"; that he constantly shows a
"doctrinaire sympathy with lovers as such," as well
as a "worship of beauty"; and lastly Spencer holds
that Ford constantly reflects "contempt for conventional morality."

With Spencer's first five points, we substantially agree. But not on the last, not on the notion
that Ford is contemptuous of conventional morality as
such. (Some who do agree with Spencer on this point
then proceed to pin the label of *decadent* on Ford,
then sit back smiling as though such labelling clarifies much of importance.)

In *The Broken Heart*, Ford shows a deep and indeed modern awareness of the suffering that conventional morality and respectability can help to bring
about. Where tragic satire is present in Ford, it is
directed not against moral codes as such, nor against
the institution of marriage in itself, but rather
against the rigidity and injustice of a social order
which makes women unfairly the subject of men's
tyranny. The ironies are especially mordant when,

as with Ithocles in *The Broken Heart*, the men are honorable and well-intentioned! (When the survivors gather at the end of *Romeo and Juliet*, before the bodies of the lovers, who is there among them who cannot claim he acted out of good intentions? And who can find comfort in the tragic outcome?)

Had Ford (as Spencer unoriginally claims) been satiric of traditional morality as such, his drama would predictably have been shaped differently. We could still have begun with Orgilus' definition of true love as

> ...a freedom of converse, an interchange,
> O holy and chaste love, so fix'd our souls
> In a firm growth of union that no time
> Can eat into the pledge....

Having first presented his true-lovers, Orgilus and Penthea, Ford could still show their hoped-for happiness together permanently doomed by the tyranny exerted by socially-conventional and socially-accepted (then, at least) forms of ambition and hatred, which entrap the lovers and effectively block their desired path to marriage. (Many medieval women, in Penthea's dilemma, escaped a hated marriage only by entering a nunnery, as Eileen Power's studies bring out.) As virtually absolute head of the family, the autocratic and strong-minded Ithocles, Penthea's brother, has and uses fully his legal power to coerce his sister into a loveless marriage with a wealthy old man, Bassanes, who also happens to be almost insanely jealous.

In obvious plain fact, any audience can see that these lovers have been caught in a social trap-situation. And can see that such a situation is potentially generative of much personal and domestic suffering, the very realm of being with which Ford (like an Ibsen) is most concerned. We can also understand that such a forced marriage was commonly sanctioned by

English renaissance morality, law, and custom; and that, for the true-lovers, there is no socially available escape. One may compare in more recent drama, Henrik Ibsen's representations of marriages of ambition: e.g. that of Mrs. Alving, in *Ghosts*, which was warmly promoted by her own ultra-"respectable" family and by the rigidly righteous Pastor Manders. Plus the marriage central in the ironically titled *A Doll's House*, from which Nora, the 'doll', willingly flees when she discovers that her marriage has become a morally degrading prison. In *The Broken Heart*, Penthea comes to see herself as a "spotted whore," in the blunter poetic speech of 17th-century English drama.

All that we have so far sketched might have been in *The Broken Heart* had John Ford really been filled with "contempt for conventional morality." But thus far he would be merely setting up a plot. Had Ford been contemptuous of conventional morality, from here onward things would probably have begun to take different turns. We should perhaps still have had II.i, which represents the sick jealousy of old Bassanes toward his young wife. We should perhaps still have had II.iii. in which Orgilus pleads with his old sweetheart, Penthea, to conduct an adulterous affair with him (which she refuses). But had Ford been a typical writer of Restoration satiric comedy, we should almost certainly have been given a secret lover for Penthea, a gay adulterous affaire, and the appearance of Penthea's old husband, Bassanes, cast in the stock role of the cuckolded dotard, treated as a comic butt.

Ford, however, in *The Broken Heart* strikes out an original line of psychological and modern tragedy. He is not imitating anyone else, least of all Shakespeare. Carefully and sensitively, he explores the real, corrosive evil that can be, and often has been, done to both men and women under the cover and blessing of conventional morality and respectability. He could not write such a tragedy of modern marriage had

164

he not seen this most intimate relationship as potentially one of noble beauty. For only then can
the opposite potentiality come into clear view, as
we see the situation in which Penthea's marriage has
placed her emotionally, as the play begins, in "a
hell on earth" (I.i.80).

With very considerable poetic and dramatic skill,
Ford unfolds his drama to show us something not outwardly very sensational, but inwardly deeply moving.
This is the spectacle of the slow, grinding destruction of fine human spirits under the pressures of a
matter-of-factly dehumanized order of life, that of
the arranged marriage into which Ithocles has forced
Penthea.

No ordinary tragic satirist could have given us
the remarkable *un*conventional scene of III.ii. In
this, at long last, Penthea's brother Ithocles too
late comes to realize the cruel wrong he has done to
his sister; and as the almost insanely jealous husband, Bassanes, cries "Incest!", Ithocles comes to
remove her from Bassanes' home. Penthea is by no
means the usual mad women of many Elizabethan tragedies. Ford is remarkable for his penetration into
major mental and emotional destructive derangements
of personality.

Nor from any common satirist of conventional
morality should we have very likely had the tragedy's
final representation of old Bassanes as a pitiful
figure, himself sharing in tragic suffering. Gradually this man realizes, too late, that he has done an
atrocious thing in his marriage. Consider his soliloquy of sad self-realization at IV.ii.17+, where he
compares his behavior with that of beasts. Only he,
supposedly endowed with reason, is the worst of ani-
mals. He himself can see with pitiless clarity by
then how his mad jealousy has driven him to "pull
down" and level in the "dust of causeless scandal"
"that temple [his wife, Penthea] built for adoration."

And we see Bassanes' plight as the more pathetic and
ironic because, so late in life, he is virtually
helpless to alter his basic character.

The denouement, the complex and artistically
controlled crises and resolutions of all the major
conflicts of the tragedy, beautifully shows Ford's
strongly sustained and modulated poetic and theatrical art. This section includes the madness and death
of Penthea; the hopeless sorrow of Bassanes; the
revenge of Ithocles; and finally the death of Calantha
who had been aware to some degree of the social tragedy of the true-lovers but unable to prevent it, and
whose first official act as Queen of Sparta had to be
to sentence Orgilus to death.

In building this complexly structured finale,
Ford clearly employs theatrical devices allowable
within the stage conventions of the Renaissance theater. Thus, for instance, Orgilus bleeds to death on
the open stage. But this is not Grande Guignol, not
stagey pseudo-goryness flung in the audience's face
for shock effect and nothing more significant.

Rather Ford uses such a device as one more imaginative, romantic means to convey his structure of
insights into tragic dilemmas of sensitive men and
women in modern society when this is dominated by
'establishment' forms of rigidly righteous social
convention and attending unreason, all of which tend
to place the form and letter of law above what should
be its essence, justice. We can readily find in today's supposedly enlightened societies the comparably
anti-human ways in which 'establishments' can operate
to mutilate and destroy all hopes for happiness on
earth here and now.

The denouement begins to take shape by IV.ii.
After Bassanes' pathetic soliloquy in which he realizes finally what vicious harm he has done to his
wife Penthea, her desperate former fiancé Orgilus
enters and accuses the old husband of driving his wife

166

to madness itself. Humbly, the much more self-condemned Bassanes *admits* his guilt. (If you regard Bassanes as a "villain," compare him with Claudius in *Hamlet*: who admits guilt only in the privacy of solitary confession to God alone, if God is listening, then brazens it out to the play's rather melodramatically slaughterous end.)

Now Penthea enters, lost in her world of madness (IV.ii.55+). So we must see the cumulative impact of her misery upon *all* the men who most actively brought her to ruin and despair: upon the desolate, too-late repentant Bassanes, who now hopelessly begs his insane wife's forgiveness and is appalled at his own cruelty; upon the desolate, too-late repentant brother, Ithocles, who forced her hideous marriage in the first place; and upon her desolate sweetheart, Orgilus, who ironically sees how mild are *his* accusations against old Bassanes compared with those which, in deep suffering, Bassanes justly brings against himself.

Ford's dramatic treatment of Penthea's madness in this scene (IV.ii) is full of sensitive penetration into human suffering. We observe what the reader may have seen or see for himself: that staged insanity is a dangerous thing to show. It baffles some in the audience, may repel others, and always runs a risk of seeming absurd if not arousing audience laughter or at least embarrassment. (This writer admits that, in *Hamlet* as he has seen it staged many times, Ophelia's mad-scenes have often struck him as bordering on the ludicrous, perhaps in part because before then Orphelia has mostly seemed a bit weak-minded anyway so that she had relatively few wits to lose.)

Ford, however, has previously drawn Penthea not as a weak-minded woman but as one of strong, almost heroic character (witness her steadfast insistence upon adhering to her marriage vows, hence her refusal of an affair with her old sweetheart Orgilus). The

poignancy of her madness resembles in some ways that
of the Fool in *King Lear*--a "fine mind fallen in
ruins." In Ford's tragic art and poetry, splinters
of her mind touch the realities of the "sane" world
from which she has departed, and they pierce to the
quick those still within it. For ten days, her
frightened women tell us (1.136), Penthea has scarcely
slept. Old Bassanes chatters in despair, "All shall
be well" (1.161), with a brief return of his rich-
man's self-assurance that aid can be bought. Penthea
wanders briefly into sanity (11.138+), guilt-ridden,
to accuse the tyrants who destroyed her: "A cruel
brother and a desperate dotage" (1.145). Then with
furious inward strength of purpose she goes away to
starve herself to death, as the only escape from a
world grown intolerable.

Ironically, the prolonged strain but even more
the sense of guilt weakens the sanity even of old
Bassanes (V.i). Is he, too, somewhat mad? when although he sees his young wife to be near death, he
still hopes medical science to save her can be
bought? Most Fordian and *un*-conventional, filled with
double ironies, is V.i. Here the desperate Orgilus
enters, having come from the death of Penthea (IV.iv)
and from his revenge-killing of Ithocles. The ruined
young man *pities* the ruined old man in his distraction
and sorrow, for calamity has brought them strangely
together. Seemingly blinded with grief, the sad older
man is touchingly grateful to be led by the younger,
as they exit. (The audience can sense the Orgilus
will now tell Bassanes that Penthea is indeed dead,
which the old husband knows in the next scene (V.ii),
where he tells the princess Calantha that his wife
died of starvation (1.15).

With the death of the chief heroine, Penthea (IV.
iv), Ford shifts the center of tragic attention to the
chain-linked consequences of this calamity upon those
intimately related to her suffering and destruction.
Onstage as V.ii begins is a bright, gay scene of joy
--the pre-coronation festivities for princess Calantha.

A courtly dance is in progress. Only the princess'
fiancé, Ithocles [Penthea's brother] and Orgilus are
absent.

In a mood of quietly grim triumph, Orgilus enters
and himself whispers to the princess that "Ithocles
is murder'd" (1.16). He then openly and proudly tells
the horrified and stunned court (1.45+) that by his
own hand he carried out this terrible revenge. Gravely courteous, he bids farewell to his father (Crotolon)
and his sister (Euphranea).

The first action of Calantha's reign as Queen of
Sparta must be to sentence Orgilus to death, which is
exactly what he yearns for. She does this with a formidable self-control that amazes the courtiers who
have been ordered to witness the execution:

It is strange these tragedies should never touch on
Her female pity.

With wholehearted joy, Orgilus chooses to be bled to
death. With one hand, he opens the veins on one arm,
in deep satisfaction that "Revenge proves its own ex-
ecutioner" (V.ii.147). When all others falter in
horror, old Bassanes, out of a sense of pity and guilt
for his part in it all, helps to open the veins in
Orgilus' other arm. Orgilus dies slowly and with
dignity, watched in silent pity, welcoming release
from life, the supreme gift of death:

A mist hangs o'er mine eyes, the sun's bright splendor
Is clouded with an everlasting shadow;
Welcome, thou ice, that sitt'st about my heart;
No heat can ever thaw thee. (V.ii.150+)

He has "shook hands with Time" and come to loving
terms with Death--it is old Bassanes who gently speaks
the brief epitaph, knowing that for himself "my last

few days can be but one mourning." For he has already
reached to understand and see himself as a "pattern
of digesting evils," and that his miserable destiny
is to endure consciousness a little longer, "continue
man still," while being in his own eyes and all o-hers'
a figure of guilt and horror. In some ways, he recalls
old Oedipus, self-blinded but condemned to live on a
little while.

    Thus Ford's tragedy ends with our attention held
by two figures. The wretched Bassanes, his "...reason
...clouded / With the thick darkness of my infinite
woes" (V.iii.22-23). And held by the powerfully self-
controlled despair of the Spartan princess Calantha.
With strangely heroic dignity she takes her place on
a throne beside that bearing the richly-robed figure
of her murdered husband-to-have-been, Ithocles. And
so she also dies, of a "broken heart."

XII   Tragic Vision--

              English Renaissance and Today

     These reflections, tentative and incomplete as
they are, arise partly from some growing discontent
with most views of Elizabethan and modern (especially
twentieth-century) English tragedy known to me. My
long-range effort is to work out, if possible, a concept of tragic vision which may be valid both for
Shakespeare's Renaissance age and for our own time.
Such an idea of tragedy might well embrace elements
of comedy, for these dramatic concerns are nearly allied if not often fused in many Renaissance and recent
modern artists' views of the human condition.

     Any idea of tragic vision offered seriously today
should strive to meet and withstand criticism from at
least two viewpoints. On the one hand, it should be
in reasonable harmony, or at least not in violent conflict, with what can be known of major Elizabethan
and modern world views. It should accord fairly well
--this is necessarily controversial--with what Elizabethans and certain moderns knew, or thought they
knew, of human nature and man's place in the universe,
with what they thought drama to be, and with what they
thought were the purposes of great art in relation to
the audiences. For instance, a witty book on *King
Lear* can be based partly on the assumption that for
this play the Aristotelian idea of the tragic hero is

Adapted from Robert P. Adams, "Shakespeare's Tragic
Vision," *Pacific Coast Studies in Shakespeare*, Waldo
F. McNeir and Thelma N. Greenfield, eds., (University
of Oregon Books, 1966), pp. 225-233.

valid. (See, e.g., R. B. Heilman, *This Great Stage: Image and Structure in 'King Lear'* [Baton Rouge, 1948], p. 30.) But one may seriously doubt that this assumption can be established as clearly known and sympathetically accepted by Shakespeare or his popular audiences or by representative audiences today. Indeed, as far as *King Lear* is concerned, the bulk of modern criticism has tended to destroy it as a serious tragedy and instead to see it in some variation of Knight's notion that it is a bizarre "philosophic comedy." (See Robert P. Adams, "King Lear's Revenges," *MLQ*, XXI (1960), 223-227.) It is a fair question whether anyone can hope to frame an idea of tragedy by which Lear may be found to be a great figure both for Jacobean times and for our own.

In the second place, the concept of tragic vision for which I am searching should, if possible, be able to withstand significant twentieth-century critiques of man in society. Some of these (the psychiatric, the psychological, the sociological) appear in the more or less formidable guises of science or would-be science. Others work from strong assumptions about and evidence from cultural history--economic, ethical, religious, philosophical. Indeed there seems a fair probability that some recent science-based criticism may end by relegating much English Renaissance tragedy to a select library of unplayable, barely readable artistic curiosities. Thus Hardin Craig's analysis of Heywood's *A Woman Killed with Kindness* finds this tragedy of sexual betrayal almost fatally weakened for our time, first, by Heywood's alleged reliance upon the "rule" of Elizabethan faculty psychology which, for Craig, does "violence...to the reasonable modern view of probabilities..." Worse, if possible, Heywood is said to do further violence to allegedly reasonable modern views by representing with respect "code morals," "social and ethical conventions such as we do not regularly endorse." Such "code morals," and specifically the value placed upon matrimony, are found out to be part of the false "heroics of bygone ages." (Hardin Craig, *The Enchanted Glass* [New York, 1936], pp. 128-136 *passim*.) It seems to me that a similarly destructive modern criticism might be brought to bear upon *Othello*. The effect, of course, is to turn such tragedy into either melodrama or farce.

My first intent is merely to suggest a few typical difficulties in the way of framing an idea of tragic vision which may be fairly viable for both Renaissance and modern English tragedy. Difficulties might easily be multiplied. Let me mention only two, both given shrewd treatment by David Daiches, whose immediate focus was on fiction, although I think his remarks also have a bearing on drama. Indicated is a problem of new knowledge and specifically of psychological knowledge in our age.

Thus:

> We now know, or think we know, so much about psychological conditioning, about the psychosomatic aspects of illness, that we are in danger of being unable to pass any moral judgement on individuals. This man committed rape or murder, but we know that he saw something terrible in the woodshed when he was three, was brought up in a slum without orange juice and cod-liver oil, was bullied by a drunken stepfather, had his emotions and instincts warped in this way or that: how, then, can we blame him for what he was eventually driven to do? *Tout comprendre, c'est tout pardonner*...; to know all is to forgive all.
>
> But to forgive all is to make it impossible to write the 'Divina Commedia' or 'Paradise Lost.' If we knew all about the inhibitions of King Claudius's childhood, we could not make him the villain of a tragedy. If we

knew all about Iago's psychological
history, we might be tempted to spend
all our sympathy on him rather than on
Othello. And it did not take even that
much psychology to make the Romantics
turn Milton's Satan into a hero.

So Mr. Daiches concluded that:

If our moral judgments of men are to be
dissolved into psychological understanding, we can no longer pattern a tragedy
or create any significant work of art
with a human situation as its subject
matter. Certainly a behaviourist psy-
chology--using this term in its widest
sense--leaves little room for an appraisal
of personality as such, and without an
appraisal of personality as such, why
should Hamlet's death be any more significant than that of Polonius? (David
Daiches, *The Present Age after 1920*
[London, 1928], pp. 103-112 *passim*.)

If, indeed, such reasoning as this becomes widely accepted, critics and audiences alike may soon find
themselves in the position mocked in a *New Yorker*
cartoon (Dec. 2, 1961, p. 64). Therein a jury fore-
man reports a verdict to a court--"We find the de-
fendant innocent but very neurotic.'"

A search for an idea of tragic vision viable
both for our own age and for that ranging from Kyd,
Marlowe, and Shakespeare, to Webster and Ford, soon
encounters another formidable problem, that of the
Elizabethan *versus* the modern hero. In a progression
traced by one sensitive critic we have, first, the
so-called true hero of the Shakespearean humanist
type, who has a rival in the Marlovian hero-as-genius
and over-reacher. Next is found the "hero as fool,"
with Don Quixote as the early seventeenth-century

"great transitional figure." Third emerges the "prudential hero" who with shrewd cunning follows self-interest, possibly disguised (even unconsciously) as "right." Of him Robinson Crusoe is cited as the "first important example," unless John Bunyan's figure of Christian in *Pilgrim's Progress* is allowed. In a fourth stage, however, that of the nineteenth century, the prudential hero is subjected gradually to a devastating critical analysis. By the end of the Victorian era, he is found to be either a "hypocrite or a villain." Consequently (a fifth phase), we have the modern novelists' (I would add, playwrights') "anti-hero"--a return to the "hero as fool without Cervantes' affectionate undertones." Thus, finally, the true hero of the Shakespearean humanist type has turned into the modern "anti-hero," and, in some cases, the hero-as-victim. But the twentieth century turns him into a target of laughter, not a figure for tragic pity or sympathy. The old Shakespearean humanist idealism "emerges as mere ignorance." What was tragic incident becomes matter for "bitter farce," behind which may perhaps be sensed rising a nostalgia for the "lost world lying dimly behind the feverish gestures of a value-less modern life." (David Daiches, *The Present Age after 1920* [London, 1928], pp. 110-112.) In this latest contemporary phase, indeed, it is not difficult to find critics who, like George Steiner, seem bent on writing tragedy's obituary while conducting postmortem studies largely aimed at a decorous embalming of the corpse. (George Steiner, *The Death of Tragedy* (New York, 1961.)

Although the views of tragedy which follow are put forward as broadly relevant and adaptable to Renaissance and modern tragedy, it may help if I provide concrete examples from Shakespeare, since these at first are most apt to be familiar or readily accessible. You can experiment to see how far our theory of tragic vision is of value for Shakespearean rivals, who individualistically explore human nature in so many different ways.

The idea of Renaissance tragic vision I wish to
offer--hopefully an idea also relevant to our own
time--involves at least these elements: the dramatic
individual's potential for good or evil; the part
played by seeming accidents in bringing this potential
to action; the effects of unclassical surprise and
discovery; the fullest realization of powers latent in
men; the role or meaning of so-called fate in creating
joy or suffering; and finally, the interaction of individual powers with the dramatically represented
society.

It seems to me that even in Shakespeare's early
experimental plays some of these elements appear. As
his insights into the human condition and his artistic
control developed with increasing richness and complexity, other facets of his thought became more prominent and more poignant. Such growth seems to increase,
albeit irregularly, throughout most of his dramatic
career.

My first point is that in the universe of men
viewed by Shakespeare (excluding minor stylized or
typed figures), an individual's full potential for good
or evil cannot be known in advance of events which reveal it both to him and to the audience. It cannot be
known to him no matter how hard he seeks to follow
Socrates' advice first to know himself. It cannot be
known even to those who are represented (like Lady
Macbeth) as intimate with the tragic protagonist. In
Shakespeare's tragic vision we find no calculus of
character which can provide, with but a petty margin
of error, reliable and hence comforting (even comic)
predictions on men's behavior when, under novel conditions which the plots are designed to produce, they
encounter strange and unlooked for situations, pressures, and temptations.

Except for some "break" in the flow of ordinary
events, the individual's tragic potential might never
appear. Real or seeming accidents may decisively

alter the course of existence, either in life or in
its dramatic representation. Not at all times nor
from all angles of approach is the protagonist vulnerable. But Shakespeare shows us no pseudo-romantic
supermen or superwomen. However secure his major
figures may in the past have appeared to themselves
or to those intimate with them, none really lacks
fallibility. "Frailty, thy name is woman!" says
Hamlet, with bitter and perhaps excessive vehemence,
of his mother. Yet before her involvement with
Claudius (and we are left unsure just when this began),
Gertrude has no dramatically indicated history of sexual corruption, of what is to Hamlet virtually inex-
plicable but seemingly compulsive "preying on garbage."
A year or so after Hamlet, the deepening of Shakespeare's tragic vision is marked in *Measure for Measure*. Before he encounters the nunlike Isabella,
Angelo's dramatically suggested history is legally
above reproach; but as this hitherto confidently in-
vulnerable figure finds an altogether novel and crimi-
nal temptation rising in him, he muses bitterly that
"We are all frail" (II.iv.121).

My second point is that to discover the individual's fullest powers for good or evil there must appear
a peculiarly irresistible opportunity or temptation.
It must come at a time or from a source or social
angle of approach against which the given figure is
found to be vulnerable. Generally, in some witty way,
the temptation fits the man at the time. Of course
the dramatically apparent "reasons" for the newfound
weakness or strength vary widely. Most seemingly im-
pregnable "defences," when put to a new and crucial
test, are found wanting. To be sure, a so-called new-
ly emergent weakness of character may in its way reveal latent strengths of a great and sinister sort
(like Claudius' talents for poisoning King Hamlet and
seducing his queen).

Third, Shakespeare's tragic vision reaches to
comprehend unclassical (i.e., non-Aristotelian) but
modern and structural elements of surprise and dis-

covery. When his major characters realize they are
in critical situations requiring decisions and actions of great pitch and moment, brief episodes or
whole scenes of soul-searching are often dramatically
in order. These inquiries are likely to probe some
variation of the question: what must I say and do
to be true to myself? But this question in turn may
involve others, such as: who or what am I? what
drives me? what are my real aims? Such self-inqui-
sitions may at first seem to pose no insuperable
difficulties to the character himself. After all,
our poet's major figures rarely lack intelligence of
some sort, whether the courtier's soldier's, scholar's,
or other. Moreover, the character himself usually
knows his dramatically represented life history as
well as does the audience--although, it is true, not
always in the same frame of reference.

These episodes of dramatic soul-searching, however, tend to confront both characters and audiences
with subtle, profound, and unexpected mysteries.
Speaking poignant but partial truth, Ophelia mourns,
"Lord, we know what we are but not what may be"
(*Hamlet*, IV.v.44). More truthfully, in the dynamically expanded tragic vision of the best English
Renaissance tragedy, we know very imperfectly what we
are and even less what we may be. A given character
himself is apt to be deeply surprised, perhaps immediately, perhaps in later moments of ironic recall
--to discover what dynamic power to create good or
evil is contained in the hitherto hidden resources
of his nature as it interacts with unfamiliar situations evolving within limited time.

Thus in *Romeo and Juliet*, Verona's composite
early image of Romeo seems to resemble his own representation of himself: on the whole a gentle,
sociable, affectionate soul, a loyal son and good
friend, of late very melancholy, no man for brawling.
But an instant's overwhelming guilt and anguish discovers to Romeo as to the audience a newfound talent

for manslaughter when he is conducted by fire-eyed fury. So Tybalt is rashly slain, and with "O, I am Fortune's fool!" Romeo awakes to a horror of discovery. Consciously, a Lady Macbeth (I.v) may feel sure that her inner supplies of pitilessness are more than ample to counteract Macbeth's being "too full o' the milk of human kindness." As she later tries in mad futility to wash guilt away, the lady (so sure earlier that "A little water clears us of this deed" [II.iii.67]) muses in horrified amazement, "Yet who would have thought the old man to have had so much blood in him?" (V.i.45). Dramatically, one of the staggering surprises for Lady Macbeth as for the audience is to discover how hideously far beyond her knowledge or imagination were her noble husband's talents as an artist in blood.

If, in the kinds of tragic vision which most concern us, surprise and discovery are non-Aristotelian but structural, consider an aspect of classical tragic character discoveries. Athenian first-night audiences were presumably fairly familiar with the already mythical tale of Oedipus, for instance. From the play's opening action the audience knew that the worst that could happen to Oedipus--patricide and incest--had already taken place. They also knew the outcome. Hence, for the audience, there could be few surprising events. For them the question of greatest interest might well have been: how would the playwright and actor represent Oedipus' discovery of what the audience already knew, the irrevocable facts of patricide and incest?

By now, of course, such Renaissance tragedies as Shakespeare's are so well known that many critics assume, I think unjustifiably, that it makes good sense, as we read or witness any given opening scene, to use an aesthetic method which was probably usual or inevitable for Athenian audiences at *Oedipus Rex*. It strikes me as it did Ben Jonson that the business of audiences or critics is to pay the utmost attention

to the dramatic action immediately before them. (See
"Every Man Out of His Humor," in *The Works of Ben
Jonson*, ed. W. Gifford [Boston, 1853], pp. 127, 147.)
Any given dramatic moment should be viewed as intensely as possible, for itself, and particularly
without superimposing later scenes upon it. Unless
Renaissance as well as Shakespearean tragedy is so
viewed, it seems to me, one is partly deprived of its
intrinsic excitement and human significance. When
the action is viewed scene by scene as the drama unfolds, an essential part of Shakespeare's tragic vision appears to be this: as the central figure discovers his true nature or potential, or gains new insight into it under pressure of events and temptations,
so does the audience discover it. What has previously
been in doubt for both protagonist and audience is
simultaneously clarified for each.

Fourth, after latent potentialities in men have
been brought to the level of conscious awareness,
having thus gained "the name of action," to vary
Hamlet's phrase, Renaissance tragic plots are often
structured so as to move toward the fullest possible
dramatic realization of such newfound powers. Some of
the oddly violent turns in his designs reflect Shakespeare's concern with providing opportunity for such
expansive movements. (For instance, he deletes from
the Macbeth source-story almost ten tranquil years of
Macbeth's rule following Duncan's assassination; instead, in the drama, new outrages rapidly follow the
first.) The dramatic consequences, after some major
breakthrough (e.g., Macbeth overcomes what at first
seemed insuperable inhibitions to killing Duncan),
represent in effect a tragic outpouring of powers for
good or evil from the depths of what we might now term
subconsciousness. If my idea makes sense, this is a
central tragic perception. It implies on the playwright's part an increasingly troubled and sensitive
awareness that such latent powers may or do exist in
men, that they are not knowable in advance of testing,
and that seeming accidents often provide the so-called
"fatal" triggering of their discovery.

It may be rash, in the course of a search for
an idea of tragic vision possibly useful both for
our age and for the Renaissance, including Shakespeare, even to mention terms of such as "fate" or
"fatal." It would be safer to say "ironic coinci-
dence" instead. In the plays, when a protagonist
recognizes a crisis, we often hear speculations, very
Elizabethan in flavor, on seeming causes outside man
himself--talk on Fortune, the stars, and so forth,
as in *Romeo and Juliet* or *Julius Caesar*. In *Measure
for Measure*, when the previously secure Angelo feels
dangerous lust for Isabella, he partly credits dia-
bolic powers in the universe with laying a trap:

> O cunning enemy, that to catch a saint
> With saints doth bait thy hook!

(II.ii.180-181)

Briefly, I suggest that it is also possible to regard
such an episode as in chemistry one may view a cata-
lytic action. A catalyst, by its presence, makes
possible transformation of matter while it remains
apparently passive and essentially unaltered. Thus,
without the presence of the passively virtuous and
unprovocative Isabella, the transformation of Angelo
would (dramatically speaking) have been impossible.
Such dramatic "catalysts," then, may embody one possible notion of a mysterious, unpredictable, inde-
terminate power (or "fate") concealed in human nature.

Finally, tragic vision concerns the complex in-
teractions of individual powers with the social fabric of a drama's "world." Discoveries and releases
of powers for good or evil rarely take place tidily
or all at once. Rather, each major reaction, like
an explosion, sends a shockwave through the society.
Each irrevocably alters old conditions and tends
fluidly to create new states of being. To explore
this broadest range of tragic vision and audience
response to it requires analysis of such states in
whole plays, working through their successive moments
of power-release and impact.

Ultimately, a tragic vision of life may not only turn out to be still an inescapable necessity but the only one that makes true comedy even possible. In perhaps no century more than in our own have the inhumanities of man to man grown more monstrous and widespread. Some ivory tower intellectuals have declared tragedy to be now dead, a superfluous means of responding to experience, an obsolete form of dramatic expression. Such declarations are at best premature. They represent the strange and absurd overconfidence born of hindsight. The writers of tragic vision today, like the Russian woman poet Akhmatova, see their mission as "to survive and testify about a cruel age" (*Time*, 23 July 1973). They challenge the serious reader to experience the fullest truths of human nature, "to balance the terror of being a man with the wonder of being a man," as Carlos Castaneda said (*Journey to Ixtlan*, [1972], p. 315).

Bibliographical Suggestions

Many will be content with the critiques I have
provided for each play or group of plays. Others,
growing interested in the questions the dramas raise,
may be interested in suggestions for further reading.
The asterisk before the author's name denotes a paperback edition. For some I have indicated place of
publication; for others the publisher, as more con-
venient.

I. A POSSIBLE PACKAGE OF PAPERBACKS (mostly). For
around perhaps $12, a good selection of critical
tools may be had. Suggested are:

*Abel, L. (ed.). *Moderns on Tragedy.* (Greenwich, Conn.: Fawcett, 1967).

*Bluestone, M., and N. Rabkin (eds.) *Shake-
speare's Contemporaries: Modern Studies in...
Drama.* (Englewood Cliffs, N.J.: Prentice-Hall,
1961). Cp. the collection by Kaufman.

*Bradbrook, M. C. *The Growth and Structure of
Elizabethan Comedy.* (London, 1955).

*Bradbrook, M. C. *Themes and Conventions of
Elizabethan Tragedy.* (Cambridge, 1960).

*Ellis-Fermor, Una. *The Jacobean Drama.*
(London: Methuen, 1953; 3rd ed. revised.
Vintage, 1964).

*Kaufman, R. J. (ed.). *Elizabethan Drama:
Modern Essays in Criticism.* (Oxford, 1961).
Very useful collection.

*Menninger, Karl, M. D. *Love Against Hate.*
(New York: Harvest, 1962).

Outlines of Tudor and Stuart Plays 1497-1642.
comp. by Karl Holzknecht. (New York: Barnes &
Noble, 1947). See comment below.

Parrott, T. M. and R. M. Ball. *A Short View of Elizabethan Drama*. (New York: Scribner's, 1943). Handy one-volume history.

*deRougemont, Denis. *Love in the Western World*. (New York: Anchor, 1957).

*Sewall, Richard. *The Vision of Tragedy*. (New Haven, Conn.: Yale, 1959).

*Steiner, George. *The Death of Tragedy*. (New York: Knopf, 1961).

*Unamuno, Miguel de. *Tragic Sense of Life*. (New York: Dover, 1954).

II. SHORT GUIDES AND BIBLIOGRAPHIES

Outlines of Tudor and Stuart Plays 1497-1642, comp. by Karl Holzknecht. (New York: Barnes & Noble, 1947: "College Outline Series.") Its aims: (a) "To demonstrate that far from being mean and insignificant, Elizabethan drama-plots on the whole are not impossibly or purposely intricate or poorly constructed; (b) to make clear that an ability to follow the plot is essential to an understanding of the play; (c) to point out that with the plot clearly in mind the reader is better able to appreciate the beauty and the wit, the wisdom and the whimsy, the humor and the pathos--in short, that understanding of the great constants in human nature in both joy and sorrow which has made the best Elizabethan drama a lastingly relevant commentary on human life." (p.iii). "In no sense a substitute for the dramas themselves."

Parrott, T. M. and R. H. Ball. *A Short View of Elizabethan Drama*. (New York: Scribner's, 1943). Handy one-volume broad view. Includes some on theatrical and social conditions.

184

*Ribner, Irving, comp., *Tudor and Stuart Drama*.
(New York: Appleton-Century-Crofts, [1966]);
"Goldentree Bibliographies.") A lot of guid-
ance for $1.35, but needs a very good library.

III. TEXTS AND COLLECTIONS OF PLAYS

Gayley, C. M., (gen. ed.). *Representative
English Comedy*. (New York, 1903-36; 4 vols.)
Has a valuable essay on comedy and the comic
sense of life.

*"Regents' Renaissance Drama Series." (Univ. of
Nebraska Press). Quite decently edited, one
volume per play, about $1.35 each.

"Revels Plays" series, gen. ed. Clifford Leach
and F. David Hoeniger (1971+, Harvard University
Press). About $5 each. This series, the finest
available, applies to the non-Shakespearean
drama all the editorial sophistication familiar
in the best texts of Shakespeare.

Spencer, Hazelton. (ed.). *Elizabethan Plays*.
(Lexington, Mass.: Heath, 1933). 30 plays.
Those in the paperbound recommended-texts are
taken from this fine collection, which includes
many of the plays which deserve to survive.

IV. COLLECTIONS OF CRITICAL ESSAYS

*Bluestone, M., & N. Rabkin (eds.). *Shake-
speare's Contemporaries*. (Englewood Cliffs,
N.J.: Prentice-Hall, 1961). Comparable to
Kaufman's collection in value, but different.

Eliot, T. S. *Elizabethan Essays*. (London, 1934)
On 7 dramatists. Almost always stimulating.
But his reasoning needs to be checked out
against the full texts. Reprinted as *Elizabethan Dramatists: Essays* (London: Faber,
1963).

*Kaufman, R. J. (ed.). *Elizabethan Drama:
Modern Essays in Criticism.* (Oxford, 1961).
Valuable collection--touches most writers.

*Stevenson, D. L. (ed.). *The Elizabethan Age.*
(Greenwich, Conn.: Fawcett, 1966). Tries to
give a clear, integrated view of the whole age,
with intent to provide background for enjoying
its literature. Brief.

Ure, Peter. *Elizabethan and Jacobean Drama:
Critical Essays,* ed. J. D. Maxwell (New York,
1974). Especially acute on Ford, Fulke Greville,
Chapman and Marston.

V.   ON THE DRAMA IN GENERAL

Adams, John C. *The Globe Playhouse; Its Design
and Equipment.* (New York, 1961; 2nd ed.).

Adams, Robert P. "Shakespeare's Tragic Vision,"
in *Pacific Coast Studies in Shakespeare*, ed. W.
McNeir and T. Greenfield. (Eugene, Oregon:
University of Oregon, 1966), pp. 225-233.

Adams, Robert P. "Transformations in the Late
Elizabethan Tragic Sense of Life," *Modern
Language Quarterly,* 35 (1974), 352-363.

Adams, Robert P. "Opposed Myths of Power:
Machiavellian Tyrants and Christian Kings,"
in *Studies in the Continental Background of
Renaissance English Literature: Essays Presented to John L. Lievsay,* ed. D. B. J. Randall
and George W. Williams (Durham, N.C.: Duke
University Press, 1977), pp. 67-90.

Bakeless, John. *Christopher Marlowe.* (New
York, 1937). Interesting biography.

*Baker, Howard. *Induction to Tragedy.* (New
York, 1939). Especially good on 'revenge' plays.

186

Bevington, David. *Tudor Drama and Politics*.
(Cambridge, Mass.: Harvard, 1968).

Bowers, Fredson. *Elizabethan Revenge Tragedy*,
1587-1642. (Princeton, 1940). Clarifies major
patterns for the type of which *Hamlet* is the
most famous.

Boyer, C. B. *The Villain as Hero in Elizabethan
Tragedy.*)Mew Uprl. ;064).

*Bradbrook, M. C. *The Growth and Structure of
Elizabethan Comedy.* (London, 1955).

*Bradbrook, M. C. *Themes and Conventions of
Elizabethan Tragedy.* (Cambridge, 1935). "Conven-
tions" of acting, action, speech; Pt. II on
Marlowe, Webster, and 'The Decadence.'

*Brooke, Tucker and M. Shaaber. *The Renaissance.*
(New York: Appleton Century Crofts, 1967).
Literary history, with many acute chapters on
drama.

Cook, Albert. *The Dark Voyage and the Golden
Mean.* (Cambridge, Mass.: Harvard, 1949).

Cunliffe, John. *The Influence of Seneca on
Elizabethan Tragedy.* (London, 1893). See also
Eliot's essay on the subject.

*Doran, Madeleine. *Endeavors of Art.* (Madison,
Wisc.: University of Wisconsin, 1964).

Dusinberre, Juliet. *Shakespeare and the Nature
of Woman.* (New York, 1975).

Eliot, T. S. *Elizabethan Essays.* (London, 1933;
etc.).

*Ellis-Fermor, Una. *The Jacobean Drama.* (New
York: Vintage, 1964). Valuable; good sense.

Farnham, Willard. *The Medieval Heritage of Elizabethan Tragedy*. (Oxford, 1950; rev. ed.).

Frye, Northrop. *The Stubborn Structure*. (Ithaca, N.Y.: Cornell, 1970).

Henke, James T. *Renaissance Dramatic Bawdy (Exclusive of Shakespeare)*. (Salzburg, 1974; 2 vols.) Supplements Eric Partridge's *Shakespeare's Bawdy*.

Kronenberger, Louis. *The Thread of Laughter*. (New York: Knopf, 1952). On comedy.

Lever, J. W. *The Tragedy of State*. (London: Methuen, 1971). Very provocative on justice and tyranny.

*Levin, Harry. *The Overreacher: A Study of Christopher Marlowe*. (Boston: Beacon Press, 1964). Acute. Has implications for a great many tragedies besides Marlowe's and also for comedies e.g., Ben Jonson's.

Levin, Richard. *The Multiple Plot in English Renaissance Drama*. (Chicago: Univ. of Chicago, 1971).

*Lewis, Wyndham. *The Lion and the Fox*. (New York: Barnes & Noble [1966]). "Over all the plays of Shakespeare is the shadow of Machiavelli, as it is over all the other plays of the Tudor age"--p. 15. Suggestive.

Meredith, George. *An Essay on Comedy*. 1877. (New York, 1918--ed. Lane Cooper).

*Muir, Kenneth. *Introduction to Elizabethan Literature*. (New York: Random House, 1967). Simplified; to 1603.

Nicol, Allardyce. *British Drama*. (London, 1933). To some, best 1-vol. history.

Ornstein, Robert. *The Moral Vision of Jacobean Tragedy*. (Madison, Wis.: 1962). Often valuable. Sometimes tends to praise plays more for morality than art.

Palmer, John. *Ben Jonson*. (London, 1934). Useful biography and criticism. Over-values the "Shakespearean yardstick" in measuring Jonson.

*Partridge, Eric. *Shakespeare's Bawdy*. (New York: Dutton, 1965). Valuable for its explanation of sexually oriented wit in the Renaissance vocabulary. Henke (above) adds the non-Shakespearean bawdy.

Potts, L. J. *Comedy*. (London, 1948).

Prior, Moody. *The Language of Tragedy*. (New York, 1947). Sophisticated.

Ribner, Irving. *Jacobean Tragedy*. (London: Methuen, 1962). Often valuable. Rather humorless. Tends to take Shakespeare as the norm, most others as deviants.

Schoenbaum, S. *The Oxford History of English Literature*. Volume on the drama to 1640. (In progress, 1973.)

*Spencer, Theodore. *Shakespeare and the Nature of Man*. (New York: Macmillan, 1965). On what Elizabethans thought of human nature. By no means restricted to Shakespeare.

*Stoll, Elmer E. *Art and Artifice in Shakespeare*. (New York: Barnes & Noble, 1965). His critical methods are worth study. Tough-minded.

*Welsford, Enid. *The Fool: His Social and Literary History*. (New York: Anchor, 1961).

Willeford, William. *The Fool and his Scepter*. (Evanston, Ill.: Northwestern Univ. Press, 1969).

VI.   BROADLY ON TRAGEDY AND ITS WESTERN AS WELL AS
      RENAISSANCE MEANING

*Abel, Lionel (ed.). *Moderns on Tragedy*.
(Greenwich, Conn.: Fawcett, 1967). Collects
modern views on the meaning and substance of
tragedy.

Cooper, Lane (ed.). *Aristotle On the Art of
Poetry*. (Boston, 1913).

Heilman, Robert B. *Tragedy and Melodrama*.
(Seattle: Univ. of Washington, 1968).

Krutch, Joseph. *The Modern Temper*. (New York,
[1956]). Sharp, on mid-20's-30's ideas on
tragedy and its social relevance to contemporary
experience.

*Lucas, F. L. *Tragedy: Serious Drama in Relation
to Aristotle's 'Poetics'*. (New York: Collier,
1962). Chapters on Marlowe, Webster, Shakespeare.

*Mandel, Oscar. *A Definition of Tragedy*. (New
York: Gotham, 1967).

*Menninger, Karl. *Love Against Hate*. (New York:
Harvest, 1962). A brilliant, socially-minded
psychiatrist's view on passion-reason conflicts
in human nature, often reflected upon in renaissance drama.

Muller, H. J. *The Spirit of Tragedy*. (New York,
1956). A stalwart humanist, who refuses to
despair for mankind.

*deRougemont, Denis. *Love in the Western World*.
(New York: Anchor, 1957). Acute analysis and
history of the 'romantic love' complex which
emerged from medieval romance to become a tragic
force in modern literature and life.

*Sewall, Richard. *The Vision of Tragedy*. (New Haven, Conn.: Yale, 1959). Analysis of themes, meanings, images "by which the tragic imagination seeks to penetrate the heart of reality-- 'the permanence and mystery of human suffering.'" Includes *Dr. Faustus* and *King Lear*.

*Steiner, George. *The Death of Tragedy*. (New York: Knopf, 1961). Learned; clever; prone to despair for now.

*Unamuno, Miguel de. *Tragic Sense of Life*. 1921. (New York: Dover, 1954). Passionately argued. Very Spanish. Reason to the contrary, he trusts passion, heart and faith as the tolerable means to survival with human dignity. Sometimes wildly funny.

VII. HISTORICAL BACKGROUNDS

*Allen, John. *The History of Political Thought in the Sixteenth Century*. 1928. (New York: Barnes & Noble, 1960). Illuminates power-struggles which often appear in dramas reflective of history.

Tillyard, E. M. W. *The Elizabethan World Picture*. (Cambridge, 1943). Details the ideas on social order and degree that the Elizabethan Establishment held to be true.

*Trevelyan, G. M. *History of England*. *Vol. II. The Tudors and the Stuart Era*. (New York, 1953). Sound, very readable.

Index

Evil' and, 70; falls-of-princes tragic idea in, 70-1; wheel-of-fortune tragic idea in, 71

Chekhov, Anton: ?1

Coleridge, S. T., 40

Comedy:

Need to lay aside Shakespearean assumptions on, x-xi, 1; as comedie humaine, 1; Elizabethan, alleged evolution of from Roman comedy, 34-5

Comedy of evil: 7, 72, 80, 140

Comic and tragic senses of life:

As co-existing in major English traditions, 4-5; as, in classic views, unable to blend, 4-5; the comic transcends literary forms, 1; comic: realistic, not romantic, as long-term attitude of English writers, 2; Comic, Elizabethan, as optimistic in the 1590s, 134-6; Renaissance in England and, 8-10: humanism enlarges range, alters spirit of comedy, 8-9; comic effects of new humanist irony, 9; tragedy tends to that of waste, 9; no clear pattern of evolution in, 9; irregularity of 16th c. growth of, 10

Corpus Christi dramas, 6-7: as medieval comedies of 'fallen' man, 7; Satan as a mighty comic figure in, 7; Satan & Renaissance devilish villains, 7-8

Cruelty, theatre of: xi, 143

Dante: 173

DeFoe, Daniel: 175

"Decadent": Middleton & Rowley, Ford, as: xii; Ford as, 162

Dekker, Thomas: xi, *Gull's Hornbook,* 12; 17-32, 135; *The Shoe-maker's Holiday,* 17-32; blends romantic with mainly realistic elements, 17; celebrates middle- and working-class heroes, 17; shows war's unromantic realities, 18; no villains in, 121-2; realistic heroiness in, 20, 23, 25-31

Devil-figures: traditional as superfluous, xii

Dickens, Charles: 116

Dickensian humor in London comedy, 17, 23

Donne, John: 144

Eliot, T. S.: 13, 38, 89

Erasmus, 8-9; *Praise of Folly,* 8; satiric *Epigrams,* 9; *Colloquies,* 9; "Man is wolf to man," 81

Everyman, 5-6; 'morality plays' fuse comic, pious, tragic themes, 5; Everyman & Miller's *Death of a Salesman,* 5; as comic while its hero thinks to fool Death, 5; as tragic when Everyman sees death as inevitable, 5-6; enduring appeal of right *vs* wrong drama, 6

Evolution (literary): discounted as major 'cause' of Renaissance comedy or tragedy, 65,67

Falls-of-princes (medieval) idea of tragedy: 84

Farces, early Elizabethan, 10-12: old rough-and-tumble humor in, 10-11; and Plautus, 11; aim not for romantic escapism but to show earthy English life, 11

Fielding, Henry: *Tom Jones*, 12

Ford, John: viii, xii, 139, 142, 157-170, 174.

The Broken Heart: 159-170; not epic in intent, 157-8; personal love/honor conflict in, 157; forced marriage as central theme in, 158-9; true love in, 158+; what happens in, 159-9; plot & character shows tragic vision in, 159; marriage--realistic & romantic in, 160; poetic efforts to reconcile realism & romance, 160-2; over-view of tragic vision in, 162; Ford not against conventional morality as such, 162-4; tragic satire in, 162-6; psychological & modern tragic vision in, 164; madness in, 165-8; the denouëmont's art in, 166-170

Freud, Sigmund: 119, 120, 121, 122, 124

Foxe, John: *Book of Martyrs*, 84

Gammer Gurton's Needle, 11

Gascoigne, George, 11-12: sophisticated humor of, 11; broadly farcical humor of, 11-12

Gawain and the Green Knight: satiric and sexy comedy in, 3-4

Golden Age, myth of, 80; Golden age man *vs* modern man, 82, in Chapman, 132-3

Grande Guignol: 166

Greene, Robert:
Low comic exposés of the Elizabethan underworld, 12; 135

'Hell': modern man creates his own: Chapman, xi; Webster, xii; Marlowe, 118, 141; John Ford, 165

Henry VIII: 'judicial murders' of, 84

Herbert, George: 145

Heroism: new modern kinds, Chapman to Ford, 139-143

Heywood, John: 10

Heywood, Thomas: x; 82, 137

History as tragedy: 24-5

Hitler, Adolph: 149

Hobbes, Thomas: 81

Humanism, early Tudor Christian, 137; see More & Erasmus

Ibsen, Henrik: and John Ford, 163-4

"Interludes," Tudor: 10
Comedy of social types in, 10

Irony; new-humanist: More, Erasmus and, 9

Johnson, Dr. Samuel: 17

Jonson, Ben: viii; xi; 15-16; 20; 33-46; 60-64, 95, 101, 106, 179-180

Jonsonian comedy:
Jonson as father of modern English comedy, 33; money & self-love as master-motives in, 36-7; as darkly deterministic, 38; as celebrating human vitality, 38; mores and manners in, 39; plots move realistically in, 39-40; styles support earthy comic vision in, 40-1; as Moliere-like critic of modern man & society, 41; the new acquisi-

195

tive society and, 41; anti-
romanticism and, 41; dispenses
with stage villains, 42-3;
    Every Man in His Humor:
43-46; makes one day's London
events credible, 43-4; his idea
that in everyday characters an
excess of any trait makes them
ridiculous, 44-5; his comedy of
'over-reaching', 45; justice in,
44; four 'humours' and, 44-5
    The Alchemist: 60-64;
as his best realistic & satiric
London comedy, 60; comic pace
in, 60; local color & the
plague in, 60; ease & naturalness of plot/action in, 60-4;
avaricious Londoners as satiric
targets in, 61+; basic idea of,
60-1; rogues' victims earn satiric audience-laughter, 61;
panorama of gullibility in, 62+;
Sir Epicure Mammon as mock-epic
greed-figure, 62+; satire on
hypocrisy in, 63-4; unromantic
matchmaking in, 64

Kyd, Thomas: viii, xi;
comic sides of, 12-13; 14-15,
65-6, 79, 85, 90, 91-99, 101,
120, 134, 136, 138, 140, 144,
174
    The Spanish Tragedy,
91-99; debts to Seneca and the
Italians, 92; novel inventions
in plot & subplots, 92; projects
recent war & love, 92; as the
first theatrically inventive
tragic writer, 92-4; as the first
major theatrical poet, 93-5;
invents the play-within-the-

play, 94; uses of multi-con-
sciousness in, 93-5; emotional-
ly-charged characters in, 95-7;
his search for a 'big' style,
97-8; achievements summed up,
98; special modern irony in,
98-9

London comedy:
    its revelation the broad
aim of major non-Shakespearean
dramatists, 15-16; net result
of literary evolution, 15;
mixes realism & romantic elements, 15-16; Dekker, Beaumont
as masters of, 17; see Ben
Jonson.
  Luther, Martin: 3
  Lyly, John: 13-14, 135

  Machiavelli, Nicolo, and
Machiavellianism: 86-7, 104,
138, 146-7; see Villains.
  Malory, Sir Thomas: 74
  Marlowe, Christopher: viii,
xi, comic sides of, 12-13; 14,
41, his 'Hero and Leander'
burlesqued, 47-8; 65, 79, 85,
100-118, 119, 122, 125-6, 128,
132, 136, 140, 174; greatest
achievements of, 100-106;
changes course of tragedy, 100-
106; his "mighty line", 101-2;
the new 'romantic' tragedy and,
102-6; ignores all petty concerns, 102-3; central tragic
themes in, 103-4; over-reacher
hero in, 103-4; passions of
Faustian geniuses in, 103-5;
abandons major humanist tradition, 104; anti-chivalry and

modern greatness in, 104; obsolete 'honor' in, 104; the conqueror-hero in, 104; tragic humor & eroticism in, 105; discovers secret of dramatic action, 105; first to explore modern tragic values in drama, 105-6; effects on comedy, 106; tragic vision of, 135-6

    Doctor Faustus, 106-113; farce & clownage in, 106-7; the comic or miraculous in, 107; tragic action in, 108-9; three large movements in structure of, 110-113; the human comedy in, 111-2; a comic synthesis & Marlowe's tragic vision, 113-8; tragic irony in, hero turns Fool, 117-8; the superman & the fool, 118

    Medicis and revenges: 152

    "Merrie England": 18-19

    Middleton, Thomas & Rowley, William: xii; 82; Middleton, 142

    Miller, Arthur: 5

    Milton, John: 3-4, 173,174

    Mock-heroic & anti-romantic satire: 48-9

    Molière: 41

    Montaigne, Michel: 144

    More, Thomas: 8-9; *Utopia* and social satire, 8-9; new sense of irony of, 8-9; on good kings & tyrants, 80, 84

    Nashe, Thomas: burlesques Marlowe's 'Hero and Leander,' 47

    Non-Shakespearean drama: mainly *not* imitative of Shakespeare, viii, x; essential to view it on its own terms, x-xi

Optimism, humanist: undercut in early 17th c., 140-1

    Orsini, Virginio, Duke: 155

    Ovid: Golden Age myth, 80; 122-5, 132-3

    Passion *vs* reason, 'new' tragedy of: Chapman as its pioneer, xi; 138-140

    Peele, George: 135

    Pessimism, tragic: 80-1; 138-9

    Petrarch: 76-7

    Piers Plowman: as realistic humorist plus social reformer, 3

    Plautus: 11-12; 34

    Plays-within-plays: Beamont's use of, 49+; Kyd invents, 94

    Porter, Katherine: 12

    Prometheus, myth of, 81

    Puritans: 19, 61,64

    Rastell, John: 10

    Romanticisms, courtly Elizabethan: John Lyly, 13-14

    Revenge plays: Kyd as their 'Father', xi; as search-for-justice dramas, xi, 91, 139-140

    Romance, Arthurian-chivalric: satiric humor on, in *Gawain and the Green Knight*, 3-4; chivalry satirized by More & Eramus, 47; burlesqued by Beaumont, 52+

    Sackville, Thomas: *The Mirror for Magistrates*, 83-4

    Santayana, George: 117

    Satan: as comic, 7; as villain, 7, 86, 129

    Scientists as tragic figures: Marlowe's *Doctor Faustus*, xi, 106-113

    "Second Shepherd's Play":

6-8; blends farcical low-comedy & serious piety, 6; blends
rough and tenderly lyric speech,
6-7

    Seneca: 88-9, 91-2, 91-4
    "Senecan" dramas, Elizabe-
than: 91-2
    Shakespeare: viii, x, xii,
7-8, 14, 15, 18-19, 21-2, 31,
33-4, 38-41, 42, 50, 53, 59,
65-7, 76, 79, 80, 82, 85, 97,
100, 104-5, 107, 114, 116, 117,
119, 125-6, 131, 135, 136, 137-8,
140, 142, 143-4, 148, 151, 153,
156, 160-2, 163, 164, 167, 168,
171-2, 173-4, 175-181; never
writes directly on contemporary
London, 14-5, 19; 'Shakespearian
yardstick' as often inadequate
for critical evaluations, 33-6
    Shaw, George Bernard: 143,
154
    Sidney, Sir Philip: 4, 92,
114, 144
    Sixtus V, Pope: 151, 155
    Skelton, John: a humanist
but traditionally low-comic,
9-10
    Sophocles: Oedipus & John
Ford, 170; 179
    Spencer, Hazelton: on Ford's
tragic vision, 162
    Spenser, Edmund: 104·,160
    Swift, Jonathan: 115
    Swinburne, Algernon: 159

    Toynbee, Arnold: 145
    Tragedy as search-for-
justice: 91, 140
    Tragic spirit, English:
65-90;
      Beowulf and, 66, 68;
basic questions of, 66-7; not a

result of clear 'evolution',
67; Chaucer and, 70-1;medieval,
70-77; Renaissance & Reformation, 78-81; Renaissance and
today, 171-182
    Tragic vision: Old English
'world':
      Beowulf, 68-9; first
tragic-hero image in, 68; no
superman, a survival hero, 68;
heroic joy in battle, 68; supreme human virtues in, 68;
supreme vices in, 68; dishonor,
not death, as tragic in, 69;
stoic tragic virtues in, 69;
no self-pity in, 69
    The Wife's Lament & *The
Husband's Message:* 69; hope
for human dignity amidst degradations in, 69; tragic vision
of struggles for happiness *vs*
the world's evils in, 69; stoic
ideas in tragedy, 69; no use
for self-pity in, 69
    Tragic vision: Medieval:
70-77
      Chaucer, 70-1; the lit-
urgical drama as *not* tragic to
believing Catholics, 71-2; was
Christ a tragic hero? 71;
Satan a tragic figure? 71; the
'comedy of evil,' 72; tragic
idea of universe ruled by moral
purpose, 72; and St. Augustine,
72-3; and the Biblical fall of
man, 72-3;
      The morality play of
Everyman: credible tragic
ideas in, 73-4; divine justice
as certain, 73; man seen having
free will, 74; radical conflicts of reason and passion,
74; tragic hero idea in, 74

Arthurian romance and, 74-7; death-marked love, 75-7
Tragic vision, Renaissance & Reformation: 79-81; humanistic ideas - a good life as possible on earth, 78; the modern tragedy of *waste*, 78; modern man as his own worst enemy, 78; new loneliness and alienation as tragic truth, 79; the falls of civilizations as tragic, 80-1; degeneration of man from the Golden Age, 80-2; tragic pessimism about the future, 81; countering heroic optimism - hopes for good via technology, 81; Prometheus myth, 81; 'great' princes & history's lessons, 82-3; *Mirror For Magistrates*, 83-4; history as tragedy, 84-5; princes' chronic wars and tragedy, 85; writers go to recent history for tragic experience, 85-6; Machiavellianism, 86; decay & fall of the world in tragic vision, 87; stoicism & tragic vision, 87-9; Senecan influences, 88-9; summation, 89-90; 1590s optimistic, 134-6
Tragic vision, Renaissance & today: 171-182; Renaissance, modern world views and, 171-2; 20th c. scientific criticism and, 172-4; problem of new psychological knowledge and, 173-4; Elizabethan *vs* modern ideas of heroes, 174-5; six elements of tragic vision to meet Renaissance and today's needs, 176-181; tragic & comic vision as inter-related, 182
Tristan and Isolde: 76
Tourneur, Cyril, 82, 87, 139

Udall, Nicholas: [*Ralph*] *Roister Doister*, 11
Underworld (Elizabethan) low-humor of roguery, 12

Vaughan, Henry: 145
Villain, the: as obsolete in most London comedy, 21-2; none in Dekker, 21-2; Falstaff as, 22; Jonson *versus* Shakespeare on, 42+; Jonsonian comedy and, 42; new vitalities of, 142-3; John Ford and, 167
Villains, Machiavellian: 63, 86, 129 ('stock'), 142; new vitalities of, 142-3; in Chapman's *Bussy d'Ambois*: 120-1, 128, 129-130; in Webster, 150-1
Villains: satanic, 7, 86, 129, 155

Webster, John: viii, xii, 82, 85-7, 134-156, 174
Non-naturalistic art of, 143; Shakespearian modes of characterization do not fit, 144; plots derive from recent history, 144; death-scenes in, 144-5, 153; 154-5; as 'romantic,' 144-5; sense of moral crisis in, 145+; Italian decadence and, 146-150; amoral pursuit of glory & fame in, 146-7; sentiments of honor and, 147-8; Renaissance individualism and, 148; great gambling and, 148-9; revenges as works of art and, 149-150, 153;
The White Devil, 148-156: gambling in, 148-9; revenge as a work of art in, 149; the heroine's character in, 150-1; what happens in the action of, 151-3;